Active Reading

Active Reading

Activities for Librarians and Teachers

Beth McGuire

LIBRARIES
UNLIMITED
A Member of the Greenwood Publishing Group

Westport, Connecticut • London

Library of Congress Cataloging-in-Publication Data

McGuire, Beth.
  Active reading : activities for librarians and teachers / Beth McGuire.
      p. cm.
  Includes bibliographical references and index.
  ISBN 978-1-59158-666-1 (alk. paper)
  1. Reading (Elementary)—Activity programs. 2. Children—Books and reading. I. Title.
  LB1573.M3916   2009
  372.4—dc22   2008025710

British Library Cataloguing in Publication Data is available.

Library of Congress Catalog Card Number: 2008025710
ISBN: 978-1-59158-666-1

First published in 2009

Libraries Unlimited, 88 Post Road West, Westport, CT 06881
A Member of the Greenwood Publishing Group, Inc.
www.lu.com

Printed in the United States of America

The paper used in this book complies with the
Permanent Paper Standard issued by the National
Information Standards Organization (Z39.48–1984).

10 9 8 7 6 5 4 3 2 1

Dedication

As a little girl, I looked forward to playing teacher with my friends. I've been fortunate enough to become a teacher, but I did not imagine all of those years ago that one day I would be writing a book that my dad, a middle school teacher, and other teachers and school librarians could use with their students. The adroit authors featured in my book made it possible for me to create interesting activities. I am grateful for their efforts and the opportunity to share my ideas about how to incorporate these books into libraries and classrooms everywhere.

I am very lucky to have a remarkably kind family in addition to treasured friends. Thank you all.

It is with pleasure that I dedicate this book to my loving and supportive parents, Daniel and Mary McGuire. They have always been there for me, and the very least I can do is to dedicate this book to them.

Contents

Introduction

This activity book includes ideas and reproducible sheets that you can use with your class immediately. Recently published, outstandingly crafted books have been selected as the topic for activities. All books have received positive reviews, many have won literary awards, and a majority are Junior Library Guild selections. Showcasing current literature with our students is one way to ensure timely issues, scientific breakthroughs, and contemporary authors are accessible to all students. This is a great time to be a reader in Grades 6 through 8, and promoting quality literature will guide students to this awareness as well. A variety of creative new nonfiction books, tightly spiraled sports novels, realistic fiction, and fantasy books are readily available. The literature of focus should have staying power with the middle school–age audience for decades to come, while allowing for both independent and class reading.

Layout

Before each activity, a teacher's guide provides an overview of the featured book, along with listings of the book's awards and distinctions, the major skills on which it focuses, reading levels appropriate for the text, the author's Web site (when available), and suggested answers to the related student-based projects and reader response questions. It is likely that many of the books will continue to garner awards after this book is published. Specific state standard numbers have not been listed because the standards, anchors, and other measurements frequently change. Particular skills can be easily matched with appropriate standards. The activities permit students to explore a variety of literary genres and read for pleasure while correlating to the American Association of School Libraries (AASL) Standards for the 21st-Century Learner. The AASL standard numbers are included, with an explanation of how the individual activities reflect a given standard.

The reading levels referenced are based on the heavily used software and program Accelerated Reader (AR). These levels are included to help gauge the vocabulary in the books for particular students. This information provides a reading level suggestion and can also serve as a recommendation guide for students.

Individual Web sites maintained by the authors and illustrators have been included as well. The teacher guide concludes with suggested answers. Many activities have student-based projects and reader-response questions that have no wrong answers as long as they can be backed up with material from the book. Answers to the comprehension questions are given as well. The key complements each activity and assists teachers in double-checking that students comprehend major points or ideas.

Chapter 1 offers activities for a wide variety of twenty recently published nonfiction topics extending from world history to social history, science to biography. Students have numerous engaging nonfiction books available, and educators have the ability to incorporate these activities into their lessons. Chapter 2 activities feature forty-seven novels that include historical fiction—tales from lands far way and times long ago, as well as places that could be just around the corner.

Consult the bibliography for more information about the books referenced in this volume. Authors' Web sites and those mentioned in activities are included in the Webliography. Use the index to look for certain topics. This is a resource book, and the text does not need to be read in sequential order.

Assessment

Regardless of the location where you serve as an educator, evaluation of the learning process is under the watchful eyes of other educators, as well as administrators, parents, government officials, and the media. Students undergo many state and local assessments each year and need to feel comfortable having their knowledge measured. Educators face the challenge of preparing students for an uncertain and rapidly changing world, and providing students with activities for the literature that they read will facilitate research skills, analysis, and creativity. In addition, this will best prepare students for any battery of testing and—more importantly—their future.

The activities you will find in this text reinforce concepts from the featured books and present various learning modalities. Project-based learning, as well as discussion, partner, small-group, whole-group, and artistic learning styles are ideal ways to present the activities in this volume. Questions cover various levels of Bloom's taxonomy to evaluate skills as basic as recalling information up to those as complex as evaluation and supporting an opinion. When I created these activities, my top priorities were to capture the essence of the books I selected, to address learning standards, and to encourage student curiosity.

The activities may also serve as individual assessments for students or as an alternative to standardized testing methods. Further, a featured book and activity display could be a regular element in the classroom or library media center.

We do not truly finish a book when we reach the last page. Truly well-written books will encourage readers to continue thinking about the characters and the situation. In Kristin Kladstrup's novel *The Book of Story Beginnings,* Oscar insightfully inquires, "When you put certain books back on the shelf, don't you feel as if the people inside are going on with their lives after the story is over?" (p. 356). The novels featured in this activity book should help readers feel just as Oscar does when they reach a book's end. Remember, reading is an active process—it allows for intense mental exercise that can stretch the mind.

You are now free to begin Active Reading!

Beth McGuire

Chapter 1

Nonfiction

Title: *Up Close: Robert F. Kennedy, a Twentieth-Century Life*

Author: Marc Aronson

Book Overview: Aronson meticulously gathers essential and less-studied information about Robert F. Kennedy and his family.

Book Distinctions: *Kirkus Reviews* Starred Review, Junior Library Guild Selection

AASL Standards for the 21st-Century Learner Standards: 1.1.4 Locate and assess sources, 2.1.6 Create a product to share findings, 3.1.1 Share findings with peers, 3.1.6 Provide source citations

Content Areas: History, Politics, Language Arts

AR Reading Level: 8.0

Author Web Site: http://www.marcaronson.com/

Suggested Answers:

A.

1. Rosemary has problems with her brain. Her emotional difficulties worsen. Her father secretly allows doctors to perform a lobotomy on her. This causes further problems. Rosemary is placed in an institution and never learns the entire story of what happened to her.

2. Joe dies in a plane mission. He was named after his father. His father hoped that he would become the U.S. president.

3. Jack (John) becomes a war hero and the nation's thirty-fifth president. He is assassinated.

4. Although bobby's mother wanted him to become a priest, he marries and has eleven children with his wife, Ethel. He takes a political route and is later assassinated when volunteering at a soup kitchen.

5. Edward (Ted) is the youngest kennedy. He began serving as a senator in 1962 and has been a senator for over 4 decades.

B.

1. Joseph McCarthy was loud and outspoken and inspired fear of communism into the nation.

2. J. Edgar Hoover, director of the Federal Bureau of Investigation, knows many of the secrets in Washington, D.C. Bobby protects his brother from Hoover.

3. Jimmy Hoffa is a major underground crime leader whom Bobby prosecutes.

4. Fidel Castro plays a major role in the Cuban Missile Crisis and was almost assassinated by the Kennedy administration.

5. To appease Hoover, Bobby places a wiretap on the phone of Martin Luther King, Jr.

6. When John Kennedy is assassinated, Vice President Lyndon B. Johnson becomes the president. Bobby dislikes the new president because Johnson had tried to smear John Kennedy's reputation during the election.

7. Nikki Giovanni is a poet who works for Bobby.

C. Responses depend on the topics selected.

Up Close: Robert F. Kennedy, A Twentieth-Century Life
by Marc Aronson

If you need more room for writing, you can respond to the following activities on another sheet of paper or using a computer word-processing program.

A.   Take a closer look at the children of Joseph and Rose Kennedy. What happened to them?

1.   Rosemary

2.   Joseph, Jr.

3.   Jack (John)

4.   Robert (Bobby)

5.   Edward (Ted)

B.   Throughout Robert's life, he had dealings with a wide variety of individuals. Define what each of the following individuals is known for, how their paths crossed, and any additional facts that you learned from reading Aronson's book. If you need more room for writing, you can respond to the following activities on another sheet of paper or using a computer work-processing program.

1.   Senator Joe McCarthy

2.   J. Edgar Hoover

3.   Jimmy Hoffa

4.   Fidel Castro

5.   Martin Luther King, Jr.

6.   Lyndon B. Johnson

7.   Nikki Giovanni

C.   Select one of the above individuals to research up close. Use both appropriate print and nonprint sources for this project.

Your Research Choice: _____

Attach your notes with source citations to this worksheet. Create a product of your choice to share your facts with your peers. Examples of product options include a poster, advertisement, poem, song, written report, or digital multimedia presentation.

From *Active Reading: Activities for Librarians and Teachers* by Beth McGuire.
Westport, CT: Libraries Unlimited. Copyright © 2009.

Title: *Gregor Mendel: The Friar Who Grew Peas*

Author: Cheryl Bardoe

Illustrator: Jos. A. Smith

Book Overview: This picture book presents personal information and scientific information about the father of genetics, Gregor Mendel. Whether discussing genes or work ethic, *Gregor Mendel: The Friar Who Grew Peas* will cover both.

Book Distinctions: 2007 Honor Orbis Pictus Award Winner, ALA Notable Children's Book 2007

AASL Standards for the 21st-Century Learner Standards: 3.1.5 Apply science discoveries to their world

Content Areas: Science, Biology, Language Arts

AR Reading Level: 6.0

Author Web Site: http://www.cherylbardoe.com/cherylbardoe/Home.html

Illustrator Web Site: http://josasmith.com/Artist.asp?ArtistID=5617&Akey=QSH5QVDH

Suggested Answers:

1. 1822, 1884

2. 71 houses, 479 people, 41 horses, 98 cows, reader response

3. tutored students

4. preaching sermons, caring for the sick, teaching

5. A universal law explains all the miracles in nature. An example is gravity.

6. Mendel's goal was to find a universal truth for all living things regarding how are traits are passed on to children. Reader response.

7. Thirty-four different kinds of peas were available, but he chose smooth, wrinkled, and yellow peapods.

8. He pollinated 287 flowers by hand. The preparation took two years.

9. In eight years, he grew nearly 28,000 pea plants.

10. Blocks/genes: each parent gives a gene for each trait

    Recessive: genes that were hidden

    Dominant: genes that mask others

    Hybrid: offspring

11. The first geneticist.

12. Three of the following responses: prevent and cure diseases, make crops hardier, solve crime, learn more about nature's ways.

Gregor Mendel: The Friar Who Grew Peas
by Cheryl Bardoe, illustrated by Jos. A. Smith

1. Gregor Mendel was born in the year_____, and he passed away in the year _____.

2. His village consisted of _____ houses, _____ people, _____ horses, and _____ cows. My hometown has a population of _____ people. (Look up state statistics to find this information.)

3. Gregor's family was not very wealthy, so to make money for schooling, Gregor _____.

4. Shortly after he finished school, Gregor decides to become a friar. Some of the tasks of a friar include _____, _____, and _____.

5. The abbot is impressed with Mendel and sends him to the University of Vienna. While there, Mendel hears about universal laws. What is a universal law? Give an example of one of these laws.

6. What did Mendel choose to prove as a universal law in his experiments? If you could try to prove another universal law, what would you select? How would you conduct your experiments?

7. There were _____ different kinds of peas for Mendel to choose, but he selected the following three types:

8. Explain the preparation Mendel took with the study.

9. After eight years, roughly how many pea plants did Mendel grow? _____

10. Define the following terms:

Blocks/Genes	Recessive	Dominant	Hybrid

11. Mendel's research was not fully appreciated until after his death. Mendel is now referred to as the "first _____."

12. What are two ways that Mendel's laws are used today?

1.	2.

From *Active Reading: Activities for Librarians and Teachers* by Beth McGuire. Westport, CT: Libraries Unlimited. Copyright © 2009.

Title: *Tracking Trash: Flotsam, Jetsam and the Science of Ocean Motion*

Author: Loree Griffin Burns

Book Overview: Students will marvel at all of the information that has been obtained by studying trash.

Book Distinctions: *School Library Journal* Starred Review, *Boston Globe-Horn Honor Book*, Junior Library Guild Selection, 2008 Orbis Pictus Recommended Book

AASL Standards for the 21st-Century Learner Standards: 2.1.5 Make group predictions

Content Areas: Science, Earth Science, Language Arts

AR Reading Level: 8.5

Author Web Site: http://www.loreeburns.com/

Suggested Answers:

1. Flotsam (Beachcombers search for cool items along the shore.)

2. Fact

3. Fact

4. Flotsam (A ship could carry 35,000 tons of cargo.)

5. Flotsam (There are three Rs = Reduce, Reuse, and Recycle.)

6. Fact

7. Flotsam (It also uses satellite pictures.)

8. Fact

9. Flotsam (They found one pound of zooplankton for every six pounds of plastic.)

10. Flotsam (It kills 100,000 animals each year.)

FACT OR FLOTSAM

Before reading *Tracking Trash: Flotsam, Jetsam and the Science of Ocean Motion* by Loree Griffin Burns, see how many facts you can identify from the flotsam (garbage).

Directions:

FIRST: Place an X in the box using your pencil that reflects your reaction after each statement.

SECOND: Compare your answers with an assigned partner. Defend your answers with reasoning, but you must agree on the answers. Place a / using a pen for your group decision.

FACT		STATEMENT	FLOTSAM
	1.	Beachcombers earned their fame by styling their hair at the seaside as objects from the tide passed by their ankles.	
	2.	Dr. Curtis Ebbesmeyer is well known for his studies of flotsam and jetsam.	
	3.	Dr. Ebbesmeyer's mother wanted her son to study why hundreds of shoes were piling up on the shores close to Seattle.	
	4.	A loaded cargo ship set to sail the ocean usually weighs no more than 6,000 pounds.	
	5.	To help stop pollution, follow the 2 Rs: Reduce and Recycle.	
	6.	Items that Curt has recently tracked include hockey gloves and computer monitors.	
	7.	The GhostNet project uses pictures of the ocean only from underwater digital cameras.	
	8.	The Garbage Patch is located where many water currents meet and downwelling occurs.	
	9.	In a seaweed sample taken at the Garbage Patch, they found an average of one pound of plastic waste for every six pounds of zooplankton.	
	10.	Many marine animals think that plastic is food. It is believed that this causes the death of 50,000 animals in the Pacific Ocean each year.	

THIRD: After reading the book, place a * by the correct answer to each statement. How many statements did you correctly predict? _____ out of 10.

From *Active Reading: Activities for Librarians and Teachers* by Beth McGuire.
Westport, CT: Libraries Unlimited. Copyright © 2009.

Title: *Pocket Babies and Other Amazing Marsupials*

Author: Sneed B. Collard III

Book Overview: Readers have the chance to visit a marsupial yearbook with sleek pictures, engaging dialogue, and catchy headings.

Book Distinctions: *School Library Journal* Starred Review, ALA *Booklist* Starred Review, *Publishers Weekly* Best Children's Books of 2007, Junior Library Guild Selection

AASL Standards for the 21st-Century Learner Standards: 2.1.2 Arrange facts with organization, 2.1.6 Create a poster and bookmark that reinforces concepts from reading

Content Areas: Science, Geography, Language Arts

AR Reading Level: 7.0

Suggested Answers:

1. All are warm-blooded, bear mammary glands, and come from an intelligent group. Their difference is in reproduction. Monotremes lay eggs. Placentals give birth to fully formed babies. Marsupials give birth to partially formed babies.

2. This fossil was located in China in 2003. The fossil was 125 million years old and a marsupial. It was previously believed that marsupials evolved in North America.

3. South America: bear, saber-toothed tiger; Australia: Nine-foot-tall kangaroo, marsupial lions, ancestor to koalas.

4. Readers can list a host of fascinating facts. *Virginia Opossum:* omnivorous, 10 pounds and 31 inches, "plays dead" to trick predators. *Red Kangaroo:* grazing; up to 6 feet tall, 200 pounds; moves 15–20 miles per hour but can move at speeds of more than 40 miles per hour. *Rock Wallaby:* grass, flowering herbs, shrubs; 6–20 pounds; hunters have been drawn to their fur in the past. *Koala:* eucalyptus leaves and bark, short and stocky, sleeps 20 hours a day because of its diet. *Wombat:* vegetarian, grass, roots, fungi; 3 feet and 80 or more pounds; child stays with mom nearly two years. *Honey Possum:* nectar and flower pollen; as long as a small mouse and weighs as much as two nickels, average life span is under a year. *Bandicoot:* bulbs, spiders, ants; ranges from .5 to 10 pounds; babies born in just 12 days. *Tasmanian Devil:* wallabies, wombats, rabbits; size of a small dog; scavengers. *Quoll:* insects; larger quolls eat wallaby and poultry; size of a small rabbit; looks like a little jaguar. *Thylacine:* wallabies, kangaroos; 3 feet long and 2 feet high; extinct as of 1936.

5. Reader response.

6. Reader response.

1. Compare the three types of mammals.

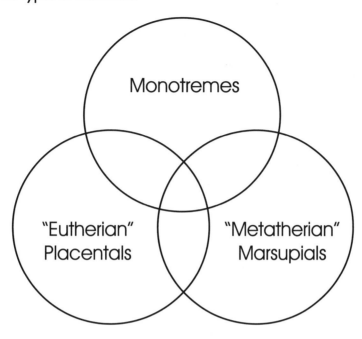

2. What is significant about the discovery of the Sinodelphys?

3. Cite results of adaptive radiation or specialization.

South America	Australia

4. Complete the following animal chart using the facts from the book.

Animal	Diet	Size	Fascinating Fact
Virginia Opossum			
Red Kangaroo			
Rock Wallaby			
Koala			
Wombat			
Honey Possum			
Bandicoot			
Tasmanian Devil			
Quoll			
Thylacine			

5. Make a poster encouraging the next feature zoo exhibit for one of the animals discussed in this book. Take notes below.

6. Finally, create a bookmark to educate others about a danger facing marsupials and how to help improve the situation. Brainstorm your ideas below.

Title: *Hey Batta Batta Swing!: The Wild Old Days of Baseball*

Authors: Sally Cook and James Charlton

Illustrator: Ross MacDonald

Book Overview: The history, rules, and terms of baseball are presented in a reader-friendly fashion.

Book Distinctions: *Publishers Weekly* Starred Review, Junior Library Guild Selection

AASL Standards for the 21st-Century Learner Standards: 4.1.5 Evaluate personal knowledge and curiosity

Content Areas: Physical Education, History, Language Arts

AR Reading Level: 5.8

Author Web Site: http://members.authorsguild.net/sallycook/

Suggested Answers:

1. Poor hitter
2. Easy fly ball
3. Played outfield
4. Curveball
5. Walks
6. Pitcher's arms
7. Reader response

Hey Batta Batta Swing!: The Wild Old Days of Baseball
by Sally Cook and James Charlton, illustrated by Ross MacDonald

Baseball has been around for more than a hundred years. Rules and terms have changed over the years. Look at the following terms and make a prediction about what the term means. After reading the book, write the actual definition. See how many dingers (homeruns) you can have.

Prediction before Reading the Story	Baseball Term	Actual Definition
	1. Banjo Hitter	
	2. Can of Corn	
	3. Patrolled the Pasture	
	4. Uncle Charlie	
	5. Annie Oakley	
	6. Hoses	

7. Which terms did you know the definition to before reading the book?

What is your favorite fact that that you learned from this book?

Title: *Skyscraper*

Author: Lynn Curlee

Book Overview: The history of the skyscraper and its social impact is elegantly presented with realistic artwork.

Book Distinctions: *School Library Journal* Starred Review, ALA *Booklist* Starred Review, Junior Library Guild Selection

AASL Standards for the 21st-Century Learner Standards: 4.1.8 Create a written and artistic interpretation of a skyscraper based on facts and projection

Content Areas: History, Architecture, Language Arts

AR Reading Level: 8.5

Author Web Site: http://curleeart.com/

Suggested Answers:

1. The term came from the high masts of tall ships know as skyscrapers.

2. The Washington Monument.

3. Students need to select three of the architects. Notable facts may vary. *Gustave Eiffel:* Eiffel Tower, 986 feet, Paris, finished in 1899, double the size of the tallest world structure at the time. *William LeBron Jenney,* Home Insurance Building, ten stories, Chicago (Illinois), finished in 1884, technical feat, not artistic. *Louis Sullivan,* Guaranty Building, thirteen stories, Buffalo (New York), finished in 1895, famous quote: "form follows function." *Cass Gilbert,* Woolworth Building, 800 feet, New York City, finished in 1913, built for the five and dime store owner in a Gothic style, nickname for the building is "Cathedral of Commerce." William Lamb, Empire State Building, 1,250 feet, New York City, finished in 1931, 3,200 people could be working on the construction at the same time, many Native Americans worked there because they did not fear heights. Ludwig Miles van der Rohe, Seagram Building, thirty-eight stories, New York City, built in 1985, motto "less is more," he fled Nazi Germany in the late 1930s. The paragraph and picture are reader response.

4. a. Petronas Towers, architect was Cesar Pelli, building is 1,483 feet, constructed in 1998 with a goal to modernize the city. b. New York City, built in 1984 by architect Philip Johnson, he helped with the Seagram Building design, this project reflects postmodernism. c. Taipei Financial Center, Taipei, 1,667 feet high. d. Dubai, helicopter landing pad near the top. e. Swiss Re Tower, skycourts throughout.

Skyscraper by Lynn Curlee

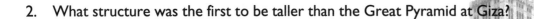

1. Where did the term "skyscrapers" come from?

2. What structure was the first to be taller than the Great Pyramid at Giza?

3. Select three of the architects discussed in the book and compare their contributions to architecture. Complete the chart below and compare the work of the architects in order to write a paragraph explaining what a building would look like if each architect collaborated on a building. Include the size of the new building, its location, and a picture.

Architects:

Gustave Eiffel	William LeBron Jenney	Louis Sullivan
Cass Gilbert	William Lamb	Ludwig Mies van der Rohe

Architect	Most Famous Building	Height	Location	Construction Completion Date, Notes, and Notable Facts

Write your paragraph and draw your picture of the building project below.

Paragraph	Picture

4. Complete the chart below about contemporary skyscrapers.

Location	Project	Unique facts
a. Kula Lumpur, Malaysia		
b.	AT&T Building	
c.		This building was built in 2004. A goal was to maintain Chinese design.
d.	Burj Al Arab Hotel	
e. London		

Title: *Freedom Walkers: The Story of the Montgomery Bus Boycott*

Authors: Russell Freedman

Book Overview: This book takes a close look at the pursuit of Civil Rights. The events are presented in an organized fashion, reinforced by primary source quotations and photographs.

Book Distinctions: 2007 Honor Orbis Pictus Award Winner, YALSA Best Books for Young Adults, ALA *Booklist* Starred Review, ALA Notable Children's Book, National Council for Social Studies Notable Children's Trade, *School Library Journal* Starred Review, *Horn Book* Starred Review, *Kirkus Reviews* Starred Review, *Bulletin of the Center for Children's Books* Starred Review, Junior Library Guild Selection, Flora Steiglitz Strauss Award, International Reading Association Teachers' Choice for 2007 (Advanced)

AASL Standards for the 21st-Century Learner Standards: 1.1.4 Locate and assess sources, 1.1.5 Access information while noting societal impacts, 3.1.1 Share findings with peers, 3.1.4 Creation of poster will allow classmates further insight to the topic, 3.1.6 Provide source citations

Content Areas: History, Language Arts

AR Reading Level: 7.7

Suggested Answers:

1. i
2. e
3. a
4. k
5. b
6. l
7. d
8. g
9. f
10. h
11. j
12. c

Activity: Individual research to the final activity will vary.

Freedom Walkers: The Story of the Montgomery Bus Boycott
by Russell Freedman

Match the events to the appropriate date from the chart. Insert the letter from the third column next to the correct answer in the first column.

Answers	Event	Date
1.	Alabama bus segregation found illegal.	a. March 19, 1956
2.	Rosa Parks will not give up her bus seat.	b. May 17, 1954
3.	King's trial in regard to the boycott.	c. January 31, 1956
4.	Jo Ann Robinson is asked to leave the bus.	d. January 26, 1956
5.	Segregation in public schools is found to be unconstitutional.	e. December 1, 1955
6.	Mary Louise Smith pleads guilty for not giving up her bus seat.	f. December 21, 1956
7.	King is arrested for driving 30 miles per hour in 25 miles per hour area.	g. March 2, 1955
8.	Claudette Colvin refuses to give up her bus seat.	h. December 5, 1955
9.	Busses are desegregated in Montgomery.	i. November 13, 1956
10.	Start of the Montgomery Bus Boycott.	j. December 20, 1956
11.	Court order for bus integration.	k. Winter 1949
12.	A homemade bomb is thrown at King's house.	l. October 1955

Select one of the following individuals to research further using databases. First write down the facts from the book and seek additional information. How did this individual change society and your life? Create a handout to share and include source citations. Choices: Rosa Parks, E. D. Nixon, Jo Ann Robinson, Clifford and Virginia Durr, Fred Gray, Robert Graetz, Martin Luther King, Jr., Coretta Scott King.

Title: *An Inconvenient Truth: The Crisis of Global Warming,* adapted for A New Generation

Author: Al Gore

Book Overview: Global warming may be a term heard regularly during weather forecasts, but without knowing what it is, why it is occurring, or its consequences, the concept is of little value. Equally important are suggestions to halt this devastating process. The book has charts and illustrations to reinforce the concepts.

Book Distinctions: *School Library Journal* Best Books 2007 selection, *School Library Journal* Starred Review, *Kirkus Reviews* starred review, *ALA Booklist* Starred Review

AASL Standards for the 21st-Century Learner Standards: 4.1.8 Create an artistic interpretation of student selected most important fact to share with peers

Content Areas: Science, Geography, Language Arts

AR Reading Level: 7.4

Author Web Site: http://www.algore.com/

Suggested Answers:

1. It was the first picture taken of Earth from space. It put into perspective how tiny our planet was and encouraged the formation of environmental groups.
2. Through the burning of fossil fuels such as oil, natural gas, and coal.
3. The glacier has melted substantially in the 2005 picture. There is not nearly as much snow as when Hemingway penned his short story "The Snows of Kilimanjaro."
4. There is a direct relationship between them.
5. Forty years ago, Lake Chad used to be the sixth largest lake in the world . The four pictures show the decrease in the size of the lake because the use of water had increased and rainfall had decreased, and because of the increase of greenhouse gas emission of advanced nations. Lake Chad is currently just 1/20th of its initial breadth.
6. The Arctic is surrounded by land and has icecaps averaging ten feet thick. Antarctica is surrounded by the ocean and is colder than the Arctic; its ice caps average 10,000 feet thick, and the land is an icy desert. Greenland is located in the Arctic Circle but is more like Antarctica. The ice averages 5,000 feet thick. These locations are similar because there are all vulnerable to global warming and experiencing faster melting because of the rise of temperature. This has also offset the balance of life (e.g., polar bears in the Arctic and emperor penguins in Antarctica). With the melting, increased temperatures will continue to rise, and water levels will do the same. More carbon dioxide will also be released as a result of the thawing.
7. Florida: Miami would be underwater. Amsterdam: the city would vanish. Bangladesh: Sixty million people would have to move. Manhattan: The World Trade Center memorial would be underwater.
8. Hotter water temperature affects coral reefs.
9. Algae, mosquitoes, tsetse flies, lice, rodents, ticks, bats, fleas, snails.
10. Using solar panels, geothermal power stations, fluorescent lightbulbs, green roofs, hybrid cars, hydrogen fuel-cell buses, and wind power.
11. Reader response.
12. Reader response.

An Inconvenient Truth: The Crisis of Global Warming
by Al Gore, adapted for A New Generation

1. What is significant about the picture taken of Earth on December 24, 1968?

2. How is carbon dioxide released into the atmosphere?

3. Compare the photo of Mount Kilimanjaro from 2005 to the quote from Ernest Hemingway.

4. What kind of relationship is there between global warming and hurricanes?

5. Describe the changes in Africa's Lake Chad from 1963 to 2001.

6. Compare the similarities and differences of Arctic, Antarctica, and Greenland in their location, how the land has changed, and future implications of those changes.

7. What would happen to the following locations if the worldwide water levels increased 18 to 20 feet?

    Florida:

    Amsterdam:

    Bangladesh:

    Manhattan:

8. How are the coral reefs affected by global warming?

9. What are four life forms that have the potential to transport diseases to different locations because of the increase in temperature?

    a.

    b.

    c.

    d.

10. List four ways to help eliminate global warming.

    a.

    b.

    c.

    d.

11. Why do you think Al Gore wrote this book edition specifically for "A New Generation"?

12. What is the most important fact from this book in your opinion? On a separate piece of paper create a sign to display in the school so that others can learn this fact.

Title: *Marley: A Dog Like No Other,* adapted for young readers

Author: John Grogan

Book Overview: Grogan and his family have an enriched life with their dog, Marley.

Book Distinctions: Adapted from the adult version, a #1 *New York Times* Bestselling Memoir

AASL Standards for the 21st-Century Learner Standards: 4.1.8 Create an artistic interpretation of favorite parts substantiated with captions

Content Area: Language Arts

AR Reading Level: 4.9

Author Web Site: http://www.marleyandme.com/

Suggested Answers:

West Palm Beach, Florida—B, D, I

Boca Raton, Florida—C, E, G

Allentown, Pennsylvania—A, F, H

Favorite pictures from sections will vary based on reader preferences.

Marley: A Dog Like No Other
by John Grogan, adapted for young readers

John and Jenny's first addition to their family is an eight-week-old dog whom they name Marley. Three children will follow. Breaking the novel into three parts based on the family's home city, draw a picture of your favorite part and a caption explaining the events.

Be sure to match following events to their location: A. Marley can't hear the commotion from the chickens. B. Marley earns a movie role in the film *The Last Home Run*. C. When dining at an outdoor restaurant, Marley crashes other tables to try and meet a poodle in the near distance. D. Marley is kicked out of obedience dog school. E. Marley has sickening times at the Dog Beach. F. Marley experiences snow. G. Marley takes a liking to the kitty litter box. H. Marley needs to be fed a strict diet of four small meals daily. I. Marley "cleans" a twenty-inch gold chain.

West Palm Beach, Florida _____ _____ _____

Boca Raton, Florida _____ _____ _____

Allentown, Pennsylvania _____ _____ _____

Title: *War in the Middle East, A Reporter's Story: Black September and the Yom Kippur War*

Author: Wilborn Hampton

Book Overview: Background on the history of the Middle East and firsthand accounts of the turmoil during Black September and the Yom Kippur War.

Book Distinctions: *Horn Book* Starred Review, *Kirkus Reviews* Starred Review, Junior Library Guild Selection

AASL Standards for the 21st-Century Learner Standards: 1.1.9 Work with classmates to increase understanding of the topics, 2.1.5 Work together with classmates to conduct a pool report, 3.1.2 Work and participate equally with classmates, 3.1.4 Creation of commercial and pool report will allow students to use technology and tools to develop their research and ideas

Content Areas: History, Current Events, Journalism, Language Arts

Skills: Comprehension, Class work

AR Reading Level: 7.4

Suggested Answers:

1. The conflict began during biblical times.

2. He was sent in September 1970. He was sent as a reporter to cover the PFLP hijackings.

3. A telex is a communication device that sends information over telephone lines. It provided Hampton a backup method to send stories when a phone did not work.

4. Children make the discarded cartridges and shell casings into toys. The three Palestinian boys are taken into a garage by soldiers. Nearly twelve shots are heard, but only the soldiers leave the garage.

5. Reader response as to their actions. The author makes three copies of his diary. One copy is placed in his typewriter case, another in his shoe, and the last copy in his underwear.

6. Six days. Israel was the victor.

7. The Black September group killed eleven Israeli athletes.

8. People of the Jewish faith fast and pray for forgiveness of their sins on this holiday.

9. This was the heaviest fighting zone. The Israelis were constructing pontoon bridges, and they appear to be invading Egypt. Reader opinion.

10. Commercial based on facts.

11. Pool report on a current issue. You could set up a digital network so students can work on this project in a different medium.

War in the Middle East, A Reporter's Story: Black September and the Yom Kippur War by Wilborn Hampton

Answer the following questions, using another sheet of paper if nesessary.

1. Hampton asserts that the Middle East poses a danger to the world. When did conflict begin there?

2. When and why was the author sent to Beirut?

3. What is a telex, and how was it helpful to Hampton?

4. In your own words, describe the following scenes the author sees when walking outside of the hotel.

   Children playing:

   Three Palestinian boys lined up:

5. If you thought that your work would be destroyed if found, where would you hide it when leaving the area? What does the author do?

6. How long does the Black September civil war last? Who was the victor?

7. What tragedy occurred during the 1972 Olympics?

8. What is Yom Kippur?

9. Hampton's boss orders him to fly from Rome to Tel Aviv. Hampton discovers a huge story; however, the story and picture is not approved by the censors. What is his story? Do you think the story deserved to be censored?

10. Select one of the following individuals to create a commercial suitable for a history station to inform the audience about the person's life. Take notes from the book and then create your commercial. Choices: Prime Minister Golda Meir, King Jordan Hussein, President Gamal Abdel Nasser, President Anwar el-Sadat, Ariel Sharon, Yasir Arafat.

11. Conduct a poll report about a current event taking place in the Middle East.

Title: *John Muir: America's First Environmentalist*

Author: Kathryn Lasky

Illustrator: Stan Fellows

Book Overview: Leave this book out on a table, and it is sure to leave in the hands of the student. The artwork complements the adventurous spirit of John Muir and the environmental impact of his work.

Book Distinctions: 2007 Honor Orbis Pictus Award Winner, National Council for Social Studies Notable Children's Trade, Junior Library Guild Selection

AASL Standards for the 21st-Century Learner Standards: 3.1.5 Apply the environment of Muir to their environment, 4.1.8 Create a nature medley and journal entry

Content Areas: Science, Geography, Language Arts

AR Reading Level: 6.1

Author Web Site: http://www.kathrynlasky.com/

Suggested Answers:

1. Reader response.

2. Reader response to what they would pack. Muir packed underwear, a comb, a towel, soap, a brush, books, a notebook, and a device to press leaves and plants. *Note that this is the list in the book.

3. The "hanging nest" allowed him a chance to see the Sierra Peak and Yosemite Falls. It rested in the air by being strung to the gables of the sawmill. Reader opinion if they would like this.

4. A bill was passed in 1890 and signed by President Benjamin Harrison.

5. It was during their horseback ride that Muir successfully persuaded President Roosevelt to establish a bureau of forestry.

6. Muir founded this organization in 1892. This is the largest and oldest environmental organization in America. Students will have to explore online to see whether there is a Sierra Club near them. The Web address is www.sierraclub.org.

7. a. 1893: 13 million acres of forest reserved by the federal government

   b. 1897: Recommendation for two other national parks: Grand Canyon and Mount Rainier

8. Sounds in the places where John Muir explored can include songbirds, larks, chickadees, nuthatches, Eastern bluebirds, common loons, great blue herons, Canada geese, cardinals, great horned owls, red-winged blackbird, canvasback, pond, bees, butterflies, mosquitoes, eagles, swamps, alligators, horses, rabbits, dogs, sheep, water, wind, or rainstorm.

9–10. Reader response. Students have a variety of recording devices. Audacity is a free product to download.

John Muir: America's First Environmentalist
by Kathryn Lasky, illustrated by Stan Fellows

1. John enjoyed the outdoors but was also an inventor. Of his inventions, which would you be most likely to use or try to improve? Why? Options: sawmill, "star clock," "early-rising machine," or "study machine."

2. If you were to journey a thousand miles by foot, what would you pack? Is this similar to what Muir packed for his walk to Florida in 1867?

3. What was John Muir's "hanging nest"? Would you like to have one as well?

4. How was Yosemite National Park established?

5. John Muir met President Theodore Roosevelt. What made this visit memorable?

6. What is the Sierra Club? Is there a club like this near where you live? If not, would you consider forming one?

7. Name two positive events regarding the environment that occurred within five years of the foundation of the Sierra Club.

    a.

    b.

8. If you would create a nature song medley of sounds heard in your area and where John Muir explored, what could be heard during the song? Try to think of at least eight sounds for each situation.

Sounds of Your Area
Sounds Where John Muir Explored

9. Create a nature song medley by recording the nature noises. Next, create a journal entry about nature in your area and write an entry pretending to be John Muir.

Your Nature Journal   **Date**_____
Create a journal entry for John Muir   **Date**_____

10. Finally, read your journal entry while the nature song medley is playing and record your entries.

Title: *Something Out of Nothing: Marie Curie and Radium*

Author: Carla Killough McClafferty

Book Overview: This biography discusses the personal and professional life of the scientist Marie Curie. The effects of radium in the medical and consumer world are analyzed.

Book Distinctions: ALA Best Books for Young Adults, National Council for Social Studies Notable Children's Trade, International Reading Association Children's and Young Adults' Book Awards (Intermediate Nonfiction, winner), *School Library Journal* Starred Review, 2007 Honor Orbis Pictus Award Winner, Junior Library Guild Selection, National Science Teachers Association Outstanding Science Trade Books

AASL Standards for the 21st-Century Learner Standards: 2.1.3 Analyze information and apply current-day situations and personal reactions to events

Content Areas: Science, Health, History, Language Arts

AR Reading Level: 8.3

Author Web Site: http://www.carlamcclafferty.com/

Suggested Answers:

1. Marie's mother is very sick and dies when Marie is fourteen years old. Her father loses his job because he is not "Russian enough." Marie has a difficult time as a young person.

2. Marie works as a governess to help her sister pay for college. Casimir, an older son of the family for whom Marie works, hopes to marry her, but his parents will not accept this because of Marie's social position. She realizes that she is looked down upon and does not like working for the family, but she continues to support her sister in the hope that her sister will help her go to college as well.

3. Through a friend.

4. Polonium is named after Marie's country of birth, Poland. Radium comes from the Latin word for "rays," which is *radius*.

5. To treat cancer.

6. A patent is a document securing the exclusive right to make, use, or sell an invention for a certain period of time. No, they do not patent their discovery. Reader response.

7. They earn a Nobel Prize in Physics. Marie is the first woman and the first Polish person to receive this honor.

8. When crossing the street, a wagon wheel ran over his skull, and he died!

9. She wins another Nobel Prize.

10. She drove and trained others to operate a mobile x-ray unit to help save injured World War I soldiers. One million men were helped as a result.

11. An example would be painting watch dials with radium or the Paris radium tea fad. Research findings will vary.

12. Reader response.

Something Out of Nothing: Marie Curie and Radium
by Carla Killough McClafferty

1. Explain Marie's childhood experiences.

2. What did Marie plan to do with money she earned working as a governess? Does she enjoy her job?

3. How does Marie meet Pierre Curie?

4. While Pierre's father watches their daughter, Marie and Pierre discover two elements. Explain their choices for the elements' names.

Elements	Meaning of name
Polonium	
Radium	

5. As a result of their experiments, Marie and Pierre notice that radium kills tissue. They believe it can be used for important causes. List a cause.

6. What does the word "patent" mean? Do the Curies patent their discovery? Would you have patented the discovery if you were in their situation? Why or why not?

7. What honor did the Curies earn in 1903? What is significant about Marie's role?

8. What horrible event happens to Pierre?

9. Despite Lord Kelvin challenging their findings, Marie proves that their discovery is an element. Shortly after proving their case, she receives another award. What is she awarded?

10. During World War I, Marie sets out to help injured soldiers. How does she try to save them? How many men did she help?

11. Some doctors and people began to overuse radium. Give an example. Conduct research using medical databases to see if there are any similar situations today.

12. What is the most striking fact to you from the book *Something Out of Nothing*?

From *Active Reading: Activities for Librarians and Teachers* by Beth McGuire.
Westport, CT: Libraries Unlimited. Copyright © 2009.

Title: *Quest for the Tree Kangaroo: An Expedition to the Cloud Forest of New Guinea*

Author: Sy Montgomery

Photographs: Nic Bishop

Book Overview: This book offers a glimpse into a scientist team in New Guinea, as well as the culture and nature of that land. Stunning photography highlights the location, animals, and people.

Book Distinctions: 2007 Robert Sibert Honor Book, 2007 Orbis Pictus Award Winner, *School Library Journal* Starred Review, *Kirkus Reviews* Starred Review, Junior Library Guild Selection, National Science Teachers Association Outstanding Science Trade Books

AASL Standards for the 21st-Century Learner Standards: 1.1.5 Access information while assessing credibility and usefulness

Content Areas: Science, Geography, Language Arts

AR Reading Level: 5.3

Author Web Site: http://www.authorwire.com/

Photographer Web site: http://www.nicbishop.com/

Suggested Answers:

1. 10. Matschie's tree kangaroo.

2. Students need one response for each category: Geography: jungles, steep mountains, active volcanoes, mudslides. Animals: crocodiles, poisonous snakes. Humans: Headhunting cannibal tribes.

3. Student selects one: pitohui, triok, echidna, dorcopsis, pademelon, cuscus.

4. Example biography: Even though Lisa Dabek was allergic to fur, suffered from asthma, was discouraged from pursuing her interest in animals by elementary school teachers, and grew up in New York City without a backyard, she continued to research animals in high school and volunteered at the American Museum of Natural History in New York. She pursued animal studies in college and graduate school, which led to her fascination with tree kangaroos and to her future expeditions. Finding tree kangaroos was difficult, but she did not give up and saw two tree kangaroos in New Guinea in 1996. In 2003, she located a safe area for the animals.

5. Readers' response regarding what they would pack. The list items and quantities that the team packed is on page 18. The items the team packed are: kerosene, pasta, peanut butter, tomato paste, cookies, lentils, ham, popcorn, pesto, soy sauce, dried fruit, sugar, crackers, rice, canned fish, corned beef, canned chicken, dishwashing detergent, salt, cooking oil, ethanol, chairs, batteries, radio collars, telemetry receivers, global positioning units, veterinary supplies, solar panel, satellite phone, suitcases, backpacks, toilet paper.

6. 11,000 plants, 400 birds, 60 mammals, 300 freshwater fish, 200 frogs, 300 reptiles. About 60% of these species are found only in New Guinea. Analysis should show that students understand New Guinea is a unique enviornment.

7. To follow the rules of their church and to promote conservation.

8. Their school experience is a reflective answer. School in New Guinea begins with the sound of a triton shell being blown. On Wednesday, students attend school in traditional dress.

9. First to radio-collar and track wild Matschie's tree kangaroos.

10. Sapling-sized sticks are tied with vines to create a 14-by-8-foot cage.

11. Tail: 21-inch tail; body length: 19.5 inches; temperature: 96.7 Fahrenheit; female weighs about 24 pounds; favorite tree: Dacrydium

12. Reader response. Tips are found on page 74.

13. Reader response.

Quest for the Tree Kangaroo: An Expedition to the Cloud Forest of New Guinea
by Sy Montgomery, photographs by Nic Bishop

1. How many kinds of tree kangaroos exist? _____ For what type of tree kangaroo are the scientists in this book searching? _____

2. There are many reasons New Guinea was unexplored for many years. Locate one reason in relation to its geography, animals, and people.

Geography	Animals	People

3. What is another example of a rare species found in New Guinea?

4. Write a brief biography of Lisa Dabek on the back of this sheet.

5. What are the top fifteen items that you would take on expedition to New Guinea? How are your choices similar to and different from how the team in this book prepared for the trip?

1.	6.	11.
2.	7.	12.
3.	8.	13.
4.	9.	14.
5.	10.	15.

From *Active Reading: Activities for Librarians and Teachers* by Beth McGuire.
Westport, CT: Libraries Unlimited. Copyright © 2009.

6. How many of each of the following are in New Guinea? What percentage of them is found only in New Guinea? Why are these percentages important?

_____% plants   _____% birds

_____% mammals   _____% freshwater fish

_____% frogs   _____% reptiles

7. Why did the villagers stop hunting the tree kangaroo?

8. Compare your school day to that of children of the village. Things to include: what signals the start of the school day? Are there any special occasions at school?

9. Name a scientific first that the team achieved.

10. How large is the holding cage described in the book, and what is it made of?

11. Write an overview of the tree kangaroo's characteristics. Be sure to include the length of the tail, the length of the body, its temperature, its weight, and its favorite tree.

12. Which of the conservation tips from the book could you try to do today?

13. Visit the Web links listed in the book. Evaluate the sources. What source provided the best learning experience? Explain.

Title: *Walker Evans: Photographer of America*

Author: Thomas Nau

Book Overview: Primary works by Walker Evans, by artists whom he admired, and by those that admired him enhance this narrative of Evans's life.

Book Distinctions: Junior Library Guild Selection

AASL Standards for the 21st-Century Learner Standards: 1.1.9 Work with peers to gain further appreciation of topic, 3.1.3 Creatively write stories based on images

Content Areas: History, Photography, Language Arts

AR Reading Level: 7.1

Suggested Answers:

1. Walker Evans captured pictures in a variety of locations that showed the reality of the times. These photographs present a historiography for future generations.

2. Walker Evans did not want to take celebrity or salon portraits. He wanted to take pictures that interested him and in which the subject was not aware of the picture being taken so that the person's true essence could be displayed.

   Answers 3–7 are reader response.

Walker Evans: Photographer of America
by Thomas Nau

1. Why is the photography of Walker Evans important?

2. Describe Walker Evans's goal for photography.

3. The book is divided into seven sections. Which section did you like reading the most?

4. Why did you like that section best?

5. What did you learn?

6. It has long been said that a picture is worth a thousand words. Select one photograph taken by Walker to tell a story in 1,000 words or less about the event taking place. Note the page number for your reference. Then ask a classmate to look at the book and try to find the picture that you wrote about.

7. Think of your surroundings. What would you like to take a picture of to place in an art museum? Take a picture and exchange it with a classmate. Have the classmate write 1,000 words or less about your picture.

Title: *The Mutiny on the Bounty*

Author: Patrick O'Brien

Book Overview: Colorful and detailed artwork accompanies this popular tale of the *Bounty* while providing a backstory to the conflict and the outcomes of the mutiny.

Book Distinctions: Junior Library Guild Selection

AASL Standards for the 21st-Century Learner Standards: 4.1.7 Use information tools to create a map

Content Areas: Language Arts, History, Geography

AR Reading Level: 5.6

Author Web Site: http://www.patrickobrienstudio.com/index.html

Suggested Answers:

1. A ship

2. Overthrow the captain of a ship

3. Nonfiction

4. Breadfruit

5. Five

6. Death by hanging

7. Forty-eight days

8. Stranded

9. Thursday October Christian (Fletcher Christian's son), among others

10. Reader response and class activity. Student can either draw the map or use Google Lit Trips. See http://www.googlelittrips.org/.

Class Activity: The map should begin from England, sailing to Cape Horn, then to the Cape of Good Hope, and finally to Tahiti. The return voyage is from Tahiti to Timor, finally returning to England.

The Mutiny on the Bounty
by Patrick O'Brien

Circle the correct answer.

1. The *Bounty* in the book is

    jewelry   a ship

2. A mutiny is an event meant to

    overthrow the captain of a ship   Serve stale bread

3. The book *The Mutiny on the Bounty* is

    fiction   nonfiction

4. They were sailing to Tahiti to gather

    breadfruit   gold

5. The people of Tahiti were kind to the sailors, and it was difficult for many of them to go when they left _____months later.

    five   seven

6. What is the punishment for mutiny in the British Navy?

    life in jail   death by hanging

7. Captain Bligh and his loyal sailors were ordered off the boat by Christian. How long did it take before they reached their destination of Timor?

    Forty-eight days   Eighteen days

8. Christian and eight sailors and friends from Tahiti sailed to a remote place called Pitcairn Island. They were marooned. What does marooned mean?

    Freed   Stranded

9. Captain Folger found Pitcairn Island nineteen years after the mutiny. What did he find?

    Skeletons   Thursday   October   Christian

10. Which captain do you admire more? Explain why you made your choice.

    Captain Bligh   Fletcher Christian

Class Activity: Plot the travel of the *Bounty* and Captain Bligh by drawing a map or by using Google Lit Trips. Key locations include England, Cape Horn, the Cape of Good Hope, Tahiti, and Timor

From *Active Reading: Activities for Librarians and Teachers* by Beth McGuire. Westport, CT: Libraries Unlimited. Copyright © 2009.

Title: *Who Lives in an Alligator Hole?*

Author: Anne Rockwell

Illustrator: Lizzy Rockwell

Book Overview: This is an ideal read aloud for a science class or for use in a cross-curricular activity. Facts are reinforced with realistic illustrations.

Book Distinctions: Junior Library Guild Selection

AASL Standards for the 21st-Century Learner Standards: 3.1.5 Apply solutions to save endangered species

Content Areas: Science, Geography

AR Reading Level: 4.4

Suggested Answers:

1. crocodilians

2. cold-blooded

3. Florida

4. Once a month

5. 1,000,000

6. A keystone species occurs when "one species changes the environment for its own use in a way that helps other plants and animals." Pictures will vary.

7. The Chinese alligator is endangered. Individual responses will differ.

Who Lives in an Alligator Hole?
by Anne Rockwell and illustrated by Lizzy Rockwell

Circle the correct word or term (in parentheses) that makes the statement true.

1. The dinosaur became extinct millions of years ago, but the (diplodocus, crocodilians, allosaurus) survived.

2. This animal is a (cold-blooded, warm-blooded, medium-blooded) reptile.

3. The largest number of alligators live in (Pennsylvania, China, Florida).

4. Alligators eat about (once a day, once a month, once an hour) during the winter.

5. The American alligator was saved from extinction, and there are an estimated (250,000, 3,000, 1,000,000) alive today.

6. Define "keystone species."

   Draw a picture below illustrating the alligator as a keystone species.

7. What type of alligator is endangered? How can you help change this situation?

Title: *Venom*

Author: Marilyn Singer

Book Overview: Captivating close-up photography and creative nonfiction writing set this book apart from others. Students can learn about species that are dangerous without putting themselves in danger. Witty topics, callouts, and quizzes are embedded throughout the book, which help to maintain student interest.

Book Distinctions: New York Public Library 100 Titles for Reading and Sharing 2007, Junior Library Guild Selection, 2008 Orbis Pictus Award Honor Book

AASL Standards for the 21st-Century Learner Standards: 1.1.2 Make predictions based upon prior knowledge to further learning, 1.1.3 Write questions and answers to support the text, 1.1.4 Locate and assess sources

Content Areas: Science, Language Arts

AR Reading Level: 7.8

Author Web Site: http://www.marilynsinger.net/biblio.htm

Suggested Answers:

1. For self-defense, to catch prey, to defend family/community

2. Bee

3. Spiders

4. Yes

5. Female mosquito

6. 50,000. It helps control vermin levels.

7. Fear of snakes/reader response

8. A symbiotic relationship benefits two species living together. Bullhorn acacia and bullhorn acacia ant.

9. Emperor scorpion. Eight inches. Three feet long.

10. The short-tailed shrew. The venom might be used to treat migraines, high blood pressure, neuromuscular diseases, and, possibly, to smooth wrinkles.

11. Aposematic colors are warning colors or patterns that creatures display to notify others that they are toxic or taste bad. Examples include red efts, western red-bellied newts, blue ringed octopus, poison dart frogs, and maroon-striped lionfish.

12. No. Jellyfish are cnidarians.

13–16. Reader response.

17. Students are to select two Web sites from the webliography to explore and then write notes.

Venom by Marilyn Singer

Before reading the book, consider what you know about the topics below and what you would like to learn. After reading, complete the chart by writing what you have learned.

Topic	Before reading, my guess is …	After reading, I know the correct answer is …
1. Why do creatures have venom?		
2. What animal venom is most deadly to people in the United States?		
3. What are arachnids?		
4. Can venom be used for a positive purpose?		
5. This insect is neither poisonous nor venomous, but it is the most dangerous.		
6. On average, how many insects and spiders do army ants eat on a daily basis? Why is this significant?		
7. What is ophidiphobia? Do you have that condition?		
8. Define the term "symbiotic relationship." Can you think of creatures that have this type of relationship?		
9. What is one of the largest scorpions that exists today? How long is it? Many years ago, how long were scorpions?		

From *Active Reading: Activities for Librarians and Teachers* by Beth McGuire. Westport, CT: Libraries Unlimited. Copyright © 2009.

Topic	Before reading, my guess is ...	After reading, I know the correct answer is ...
10. There is one venomous mammal in North America. What is it called? How might it have a positive impact?		
11. What purpose do aposematic colors serve? What creatures use these colors?		
12. Are jellyfish actually a fish? If not, what are they?		

Your turn: Come up with four different topics and locate the correct answer. Try to stump your classmates with your topics.

Your question	Guess from a classmate	Correct answer
13.		
14.		
15.		
16.		

17. Marilyn Singer consulted numerous books and Web sites for her research. Select one of the Web sites to further explore.

Web site	Notes

Title: *The Ultimate Weapon: A Race to Develop the Atomic Bomb*

Author: Edward T. Sullivan

Book Overview: Primary photographs and writings enhance the organized research about the social, political, and international effects of the time during the creation of the atomic bomb.

Book Distinctions: 2007 Parents' Choice Silver Honor Book, 2008 Outstanding Science Trade Book for Students K–12: National Science, Teachers Association-Children's Book Council

AASL Standards for the 21st-Century Learner Standards: 4.1.8 Create a poem and billboard to express ideas and events during this time period

Content Areas: History, Language Arts

AR Reading Level: 9.5

Author Web Site: http://www.sully-writer.com/

Suggested Answers:

1. Leo Szilard saw a need for the United States to have a nuclear research program. He asked his respected friend Albert Einstein to help convince other leaders. Einstein wrote a letter to warn President Roosevelt of the threat of nuclear weapons being developed by the Nazis. In 1939, Roosevelt formed the committee, and funding began in the late 1940s.

2. It was a competitive race to develop an atomic bomb. It was secretive because scientists and politicians did not want other countries to learn about U.S. research and plans.

3. Poetry is reader response but needs to be supported by facts.

4. Reader response.

5. The bomb project was intended to prevent Nazi Germany from gaining more power. Japan was not known to have nuclear capabilities. Sixty-nine scientists signed a petition concluding that it would be unjust to bomb Japan because the devastation would be too much.

6. Truman made the final decision to drop the bomb. Truman knew that thousands of American soldiers were dying in their fight against the Japanese. The bomb cost $2 billion to develop, and using it against Japan would save American lives. He did not think that directly warning Japan about the bomb would be an effective strategy. The explanation is reader response.

The Ultimate Weapon: A Race to Develop the Atomic Bomb
by Edward T. Sullivan

1. What events led to the formation of the Advisory Committee on Uranium by President Franklin D. Roosevelt?

2. What was the Manhattan Project, and why was it top secret?

3. Choose one of the secret cities (Hanford, Los Alamos, or Oak Ridge) and compose a poem about people's lives there during the Manhattan Project. Be sure to mention the city in your writing.

4. Look at the signs found on page 59 illustrating the importance of secrecy. Which billboard is most convincing to you? If you were to design a billboard for present-day America and the importance of secrecy, what would it look like? Draw a picture on the back of this sheet.

5. Elaborate on the "moral consequences" for the scientists involved in the Trinity Test and Manhattan Project.

6. What role did President Truman play in the history of the atomic bomb? Would you make the same decisions as Truman? Explain.

Title: *Team Moon: How 400,000 People Landed Apollo 11 on the Moon*

Author: Catherine Thimmesh

Book Overview: A "wowing"-type of book complete with photographs and firsthand accounts that puts the massive project of landing a person on the moon into perspective.

Book Distinctions: 2007 Robert Sibert Medal Book, YALSA Best Book for Young Adults, 2007 Honor Orbis Pictus Award Winner, American Library Association 2007 Notable Children's Books, Junior Library Guild Selection, *School Library Journal* Starred Review, *Publishers Weekly* Starred Review, National Science Teachers Association Outstanding Science Trade Books

AASL Standards for the 21st-Century Learner Standards: 1.1.2 Make predictions based upon prior knowledge to further learning, 4.1.8 Create a new mission patch and explain their design

Content Areas: Science, History, Language Arts

AR Reading Level: 7.5

Author Web Site: http://www.catherinethimmesh.com/

Suggested Answers:

1. 12 minutes

2. Just over 11 minutes

3. About 500 individuals

4. Bad winds on planet Earth

5. 2.5 million hours

6. No

7. July 24, 1969

8. Yes

9. The image of the eagle is not only aligned to the lunar module but is also the symbol of the United States of America. The eagle grasps an olive branch to reflect the peace in the space mission. Also, the Apollo 11 mission patch acknowledges the group effort by not listing the names of the astronauts, which had been past practice. This way, the first moon landing is credited to all the people involved.

10. Reader response.

Team Moon: How 400,000 People Landed Apollo 11 on the Moon
by Catherine Thimmesh

Before reading, make a prediction for each question that follows. Then as you read, write the answer from the book in the appropriate place on your moon chart.

Prediction	Question	Actual Answer
	1. How many minutes worth of fuel was provided for the landing on the moon?	
	2. How long did the landing on the moon take?	
	3. Estimate how many individuals were involved in the space suit design.	
	4. What almost stopped viewers from seeing TV images of the landing?	
	5. Provide the estimate of how many man hours it took to create the portable life support system.	
	6. Were the astronauts allowed to keep souvenirs from the moon for themselves?	
	7. On what date did the first man walk on the moon?	
	8. Was there a fear of moon bugs?	

9. What are three symbolic aspects of the Apollo 11 mission patch?

10. Buzz Aldrin would like to see a "human footprint upon Martian soil." Create a patch for a mission to Mars. Explain your symbolism.

From *Active Reading: Activities for Librarians and Teachers* by Beth McGuire.
Westport, CT: Libraries Unlimited. Copyright © 2009.

Title: *Hurricane Force: In the Path of America's Deadliest Storms*

Author: Joseph B. Treaster

Book Overview: Colorful photographs, firsthand reporting, and quotes from eye-witness sources outline the devastation that has been caused by hurricanes.

Book Distinctions: ALA *Booklist* Starred Review, *School Library Journal* Starred Review, Junior Library Guild Selection

AASL Standards for the 21st-Century Learner Standards: 1.1.7 Analyze facts from a variety of sources to remove biased comments, 2.1.4 Apply technology and resources to arrange and display knowledge.

Content Areas: Science, Geography, History, Language Arts

AR Reading Level: 8.3

Suggested Answers:

1. August 2005, southern Louisiana, Mississippi coast, 1,800 lives, $135 billion in damage

2. Hurakan/Taino, Carib, Arawak Indians name for an evil god/ huracan

3. Hurricane season

4. Tiros = Television Infrared Observation Satellite, GOES = Geostationary Operational Environmental Satellite. Reader response.

5. To show naysayers the strength of their aircraft. Next answer is reader response.

6. 1950: international phonetic code is used. 1954: hurricanes are given women's names. 1979: Men's names are now used as well. New plan: reader response.

7. a) Global warming. b) Alternating cycles of high and low hurricane activity.

8. Category 5: winds greater than 155 miles per hour, storm surge at 18 feet, possible catastrophic damage. The three Category 5 hurricanes are (a) Galveston Hurricane of 1900, Texas; (b) Labor Day Hurricane of 1935, Florida Keys hit; (c) Gilbert, 1988, Belize.

9. People did not have enough shelter to go to, stores and homes were looted, there was not enough food and drinkable water. Government officials requested 40,000 troops but only received a maximum of 16,000 troops.

Hurricane Force: In the Path of America's Deadliest Storms
by Joseph B. Treaster

1. Create a fact card about the occurrence of Hurricane Katrina. Locate your picture from CNN (www.CNN.com), recognized for their excellence in covering the event with the Peabody Award in 2006.

Hurricane Katrina
   Date:
   Areas hit:
   Lives lost:
   Monetary damage:	

2. Write about the word history of "hurricane." Provide the foreign word in the empty spaces of the left-hand column, or the source of the word in the right-hand column.

	Mayan god of big wind
Hurican	
	Spanish word

3. What is the period from June 1 to November 30 known as?

4. Define Tiros and Goes. Which system would you rather use? Why?

Abbreviation	Name	Definition
Tiros	Television Infrared Observation Satellite	
Goes	Geostationary Operational Environmental Satellite	

5. Colonel Joseph B. Duckworth flew an AT-6 plane into a hurricane in 1943. Why did he do this? Would you have chosen to fly through a hurricane if you were in Duckworth's situation? Why or why not?

6. How has the naming process of hurricanes changed over the years?

1950	1953	1979

Propose a new plan for naming hurricanes.

7. What are two possible explanations for the recent increase in storms?

    a.

    b.

8. Provide a definition for the most dangerous category of hurricane.

Three Atlantic hurricanes measured into this category. Where and when did the hurricanes take place?

    a.

    b.

    c.

9. What were some of the difficulties that the residents and local and U.S. government officials faced during and after Hurricane Katrina? Make a chart to portray the problems.

Hint: The Hurricane Katrina Timeline in the book will be very helpful.

From *Active Reading: Activities for Librarians and Teachers* by Beth McGuire.
Westport, CT: Libraries Unlimited. Copyright © 2009.

Chapter 2

Fiction

Title: *The Golden Dream of Carlo Chuchio*

Author: Lloyd Alexander

Book Overview: Take the journey of a lifetime with Carlo in this book crafted with exquisite settings and lively characters, not to mention enticing chapter endings.

Book Distinctions: *Publishers Weekly* Best Children's Books of 2007, Junior Library Guild Selection, ALA *Booklist* Starred Review, *Publishers Weekly Review* Starred Review, *Horn Book* Starred Review

AASL Standards for the 21st-Century Learner Standards: 4.1.2 Reflect upon character choices compared to their own

Content Areas: Language Arts

AR Reading Level: 4.6

Suggested Answers:

1. Carlo sees an unfamiliar bookseller. The bookseller suggests that Carlo might like to read an adventure book. Carlo does not have money for the book, but the merchant does not make him pay. When reading the book, Carlo notices a piece of parchment.

2. Reader response.

3. They find the location according to the map, but to dig for the treasure, they would have to destroy the caravanserai. They choose not to destroy it.

4. **People:**

Carlo: Carlo's parents have died, so his uncle becomes his guardian. Carlo loves to read and daydream. He works for his uncle.

Uncle Evariste: After Carlo messes up a large account, Uncle Evariste fires him.

Baksheesh: This character wants to be Carlo's servant. Carlo learns Baksheesh was a thief. If he is caught, Baksheesh will be punished by having body parts cut off. He gets Carlo out of some jams, but telling Bashir that Carlo is Chooch Mirza Crown Prince of Ferenghi-Land creates problems.

Shira: Previously disguised as a boy named Rabbit, Shira will be Carlo's assistant. Her goal is to return to her home.

Charkosh: Charkosh attacked Shira's family. He ran a slave trade operation, but Shira escaped from him

Salamon: He finds wealth to be a burden. Insightful, he finds the world itself to be the very best school.

Chesmin Khabib: A seller at the Bazaar of Dreams who tells the travelers what their dreams are.

Bashir: Bashir is the leader of the Bashi-Bazouks, who are nomad horse breeders.

Zuski the cockroach: A warlord.

Kuchik: Shira's brother, who is still alive.

Dashtani: A servant who falls in love with Baksheesh.

Places:

Magenta: Carlo's home at the start of the story.

Sidya: Carlo gets a free ride to Sidya, but he gets seasick en route. Sidya is a bustling town and the doorstep to Golden Dreams.

Marakand: Across the sea from Magenta, Marakand is the gateway to Golden Dreams.

Shahryar-eh-Ghermezi: This is smaller town; the friends visit the Bazaar of Dreams there.

Talaya: This is the little town that Sira used to know so well, but it is not as nice as she remembered.

Road of the Golden Dreams: The destination indicated on the map.

The Golden Dream of Carlo Chuchio
by Lloyd Alexander

1. How does Carlo end up with a treasure map?

2. Would you follow the map? Why or why not?

3. Does Carlo find the treasure? Explain your answer.

4. Get ready! There is no picture in the book of the map that Carlo had. Think of how you would draw a map for a reader to follow the development of characters and places visited. Be sure to include the people and locations listed below. You may add additional characters and places. *People to include in the map:* Carlo, Uncle Evariste, Baksheesh, Shira, Charkosh, Salamon, Chesmin Khabib, Bashir, Zuski-the-Cockroach, Kuchik, Dashtani. *Locations to include on the map:* Magenta, Sidya, Marakand, Shahryar-eh-Ghermezi, Talaya, Road of the Golden Dreams.

From *Active Reading: Activities for Librarians and Teachers* by Beth McGuire.
Westport, CT: Libraries Unlimited. Copyright © 2009.

Title: *One-Handed Catch*

Author: M. J. Auch

Book Overview: A meaningful and easy-to-relate-to book about what it means not to give up. The historical fiction setting of the novel adds depth to the plot.

Book Distinctions: Junior Library Guild Selection

AASL Standards for the 21st-Century Learner Standards: 2.1.4 Apply technology and resources to arrange and display knowledge

Content Areas: Language Arts, History, Physical Education

AR Reading Level: 4.2

Author Web Site: http://mjauch.com/

Suggested Answers:

1. July 4, 1946

2. His left hand gets stuck in a meat cutter at his family's butcher shop.

3. Play baseball

4. His mom wants him to learn to do things on his own. Dad is very upset by the event and rarely makes jokes anymore.

5. A right-hand baseball glove that belonged to the man's son. His son died in battle before VJ Day.

6. This was the first time that he could get new shoes since the ration. Tank factories became the focus rather than cars. Collections were held for cooking fat to make other products. Candy companies had to limit production.

7. Ted Williams was a professional baseball player. He batted left handed to be closer to the base. Norm decides to bat left handed even though he does not have a left hand.

8. Yes, he pitches in a difficult game and strikes out the first batter. He does not give in to adversity. Reader response for Norm's card.

9. The students' cards are based on research of a selected player.

One-Handed Catch by M. J. Auch

The war is finally over, and rations have been lifted in this historical fiction novel, *One-Handed Catch*. Answer the following questions.

1. On what date is 12-year-old Norm's life changed forever? _____

2. What is the event that takes place? _____

_____

_____

_____

_____

3. Even though this horrible event occurs, what does Norm still hope to do?

_____

_____

_____

_____

4. Compare how Norm's mom and dad handle the accident.

_____

_____

_____

_____

5. Norm helps a man carry groceries and receives a special tip. What is he given?

_____

_____

_____

_____

6. How were the following things affected by rationing during the war?

Shoes_____

Cars_____

Cooking fat _____

Halloween _____

7. Who was Ted Williams, and what impact did he have on Norm?

_____

_____

_____

8. Does Norm's work pay off? Explain.

_____

_____

_____

9. If you were to make a baseball card for Norm, what information would you include?

_____

_____

_____

Research one of the following baseball players by using print resources, databases and the Baseball Hall of Fame website: www.baseballhalloffame.org. Gather your information to make a baseball card highlighting their determination. Choices for research are Jim Abbott, Mordecai Brown, Pete Gray, or Burt Shepard.

Front of Card (include name, team, position, year)	Back of Card (include statistics, evidence of determination, life after baseball, neat facts)

Title: *The Traitor's Gate: A Novel*

Author: Avi

Illustrator: Karina Raude

Book Overview: Drama and reasons for distrust follow John as he tries to raise money to get his father and family out of debt in this novel taking place in London in 1849.

Book Distinctions: *School Library Journal* Starred Review, Junior Library Guild Selection

AASL Standards for the 21st-Century Learner Standards: 3.1.3 Demonstrate an understanding of the novel in both writing and speaking

Content Area: Language Arts

AR Reading Level: 5.1

Author Web Site: http://www.avi-writer.com/

Illustrator Web Site: http://karinaraude.com/index.html

Suggested Answers

The rating of characters' trustworthiness is a reader's choice, but decisions need to be supported by incidents from the novel.

Wesley John Louis Huffman: John's dad

Leticia Huffman: John's mom

Clarissa Huffman: John's sister

John Horatio Huffman: main character

Bridgit: servant to the Huffman family

Sergeant Muldspoon: teacher

Jean Farquatt: Leticia's suitor

Lady Euphemia: John's great-great aunt

Inspector Copperfield: informant

Sary: street urchin, also a sneak

William (Wilkie): butler to great-great aunt

Connop Nottingham: actor

Jeremiah Snugsbe: church worker

The Traitor's Gate: A Novel
by Avi, illustrated by Karina Raude

Task: An outside detective is needed to identify the worst traitor from Avi's book. Before selecting the worst traitor, you will have to decide how much you trust each character from the book and evaluate his or her actions. In the character chart, write about the character and his or her actions that were or were not admirable. The last two boxes allow you to select the most innocent and most traitorous characters. Prepare your verdicts as a speech to the class.

Character	Rank Level of Trust (1–13, with 1 being most trustworthy)	Background/Actions
Wesley John Louis Huffman		
Leticia Huffman		
Clarissa Huffman		
John Horatio Huffman		
Bridgit		
Sergeant Muldspoon		
Jean Farquatt		
Lady Euphemia		
Inspector Copperfield		
Sary		
William (Wilkie)		
Connop Nottingham		
Jeremiah Snugsbe		

From *Active Reading: Activities for Librarians and Teachers* by Beth McGuire. Westport, CT: Libraries Unlimited. Copyright © 2009.

Title: *Framed*

Author: Frank Cottrell Boyce

Book Overview: A mix of art, facts, and crime create a fantastic children's book.

Book Distinctions: American Library Association 2007 Notable Children's Books, *Publishers Weekly* Review Starred Review, *School Library Journal* Starred Review, *Kirkus Reviews* Starred Review, *School Library Journal* Best Books 2006, Junior Library Guild Selection, *Bulletin of the Center for Children's Books* Starred Review

AASL Standards for the 21st-Century Learner Standards: 1.1.8 Skillfully use and locate print and nonprint resources to further their research project, 4.1.8 Create a recipe using the information about the artists

Content Areas: Art, Family Consumer Sciences

AR Reading Level: 4.2

Suggested Answers:

1. At the start of the novel, they own Snowdonia Oasis Auto Marvel and Copier Center, which is primarily a gas station.

2. The story takes place in Manod, a very small city.

3. Lester thinks that the hens are named after great Italian artists, but they are actually named after the Teenage Mutant Ninja Turtles.

4. Titian Tart, Tintoretto Turnover, Crispy Choc Constables

5. Many artists are included in the novel. Students may select from Leonard da Vinci, Michelangelo, Luis Melendez, Quentin Massys, Pierre-Auguste Renoir, Henriette Browne, Jan van Eyck, Claude Monet, Hans Holbein the Younger, Vincent van Gogh

Framed by Frank Cottrell Boyce

1. What type of business does Dylan's family own?

   _____

2. Where does the story take place? What is the size of the city?

   _____

3. Lester hears that the hens are named Donatello, Michelangelo, Raphael, and Leonardo. How does he think the hens received these names? What is the real reason for their names?

4. The family tries to make their store unique for their customers. One such effort is to make desserts inspired by art. What are three desserts they made?

   _____

5. Choose an artist that interests you who is also mentioned in the book. Learn essential facts about the artist and design a cake based on his or her work. Consult print and nonprint sources. Be sure to visit the National Gallery Online currently at www.nationalgallery.org.uk.

   Artist: _____ Birth date: _____

   Most famous works: _____

   Your cake title: _____

   Recipe:

   _____

   _____

   _____

   _____

   _____

   _____

Cake illustration: Draw your cake on the back of this sheet or a separate piece of paper.

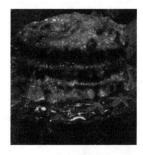  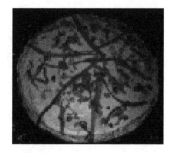

From *Active Reading: Activities for Librarians and Teachers* by Beth McGuire.
Westport, CT: Libraries Unlimited. Copyright © 2009.

Title: *Atherton: The House of Power*

Author: Patrick Carman

Book Overview: Searching for an item that his father had hid for him years ago, Edgar finds a book, but this only leads to more confusion. In his journey to find answers, he meets new friends and travels to unfamiliar locations.

Book Distinctions: Junior Library Guild Selection, Voice of Youth Advocates 2007 Top Shelf Fiction for Middle School Readers

AASL Standards for the 21st-Century Learner Standards: 4.1.5 Evaluate personal response to ideas from the book

Content Areas: Language Arts, Agriculture

AR Reading Level: 6.1

Author Web Site: http://www.patrickcarman.com/main/index.html

Suggested Answers:

1. Highlands: Samuel, Sir Emerik, Lord Phineus; Tabletop: Edgar, Mr. Ratikan, Isabel; Flatlands: Cleaners, Vincent, Luther Kincaid

2. Reader response.

3. The friend option is a reader response, but a common response might be Isabel because she helps keep secrets and makes slingshots. Samuel also keeps secrets to help Edgar, and he helps him with reading.

4. Figs are exchanged to the Highlands in return for water. They are valuable, because only one-tenth of their figs stay in the village. Villagers use the figs to sling at enemies.

5. Dr. Harding is a scientist who helps create this new world of Atherton.

Atherton: The House of Power
by Patrick Carman

1. Where do the following characters live for the majority of the story?

   Edgar, Vincent, Mr. Ratikan, Samuel, Cleaners, Isabel, Sir Emerik, Luther Kincaid, Lord Phineus

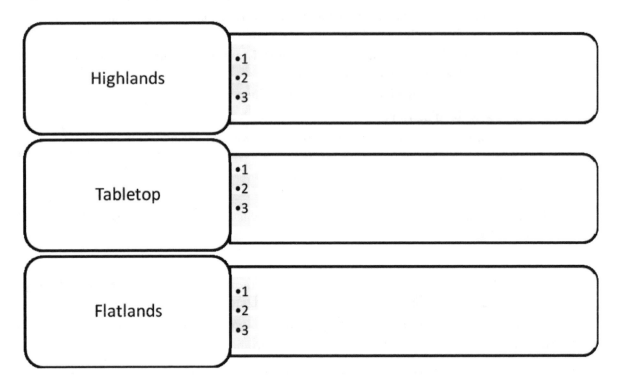

2. In which land would you like to live as it is described at the beginning of the book? Why?

3. Edgar spends his life as an orphan, or an orchard boy. He often feels lonely, but as the story progresses, he makes several friends. Select one of Edgar's new friends and write about their friendship.

4. What is the significance of the figs?

5. Who is Dr. Harding? What role does he have to play with Atherton?

Title: *Open Court*

Author: Carol Clippinger

Book Overview: How far can you push your talents, while still having a good time?

Book Distinctions: Junior Library Guild Selection

AASL Standards for the 21st-Century Learner Standards: 4.1.7 Use appropriate tools to create a poster

Content Areas: Language Arts, Physical Education, Guidance

AR Reading Level: 3.8

Suggested Answers:

1. Reader response.

2. Janie has a metal breakdown and is in the hospital. Reader response for the rest of the question.

3. Polly attends a math camp.

4. Reader response.

5. Luke stole an important object that belongs to her coach.

6. This is a first-class tennis academy. It shows Hall that her parents are very serious about her future in tennis.

7. Creative postcard design and interpretation. Students can also be given the option to create a postcard using computer and Internet resources. After registering for a free account, students can create a postcard at www.smilebox.com.

1. Hall's best friend Eve seems to becoming distant. What reasons do you think account for their drifting friendship?

2. What happens to Hall's tennis partner, Janie? Do you think that she will get better? Will she ever play tennis again?

3. Polly is very talented. What type of camp does she attend in the summer?

4. If you could select a type of camp to attend, what would it be? Why?

5. Hall has her coach Trent drive her to Luke's house. Why does she do this?

6. What is the significance of Hall and her mother going to visit Bickford?

7. If you were Trent, would you want Hall to attend Bickford? Pretend you are Trent and write Hall a postcard sent to Bickford. Design the front of a postcard that captures Trent's personality. The back of the postcard will have the message from Trent. Be sure to create a postage stamp and a mailing address to Hall. You can also create a caption to describe the front image on the back of the postcard. Cut out the postcard halves and glue together.

Front of the postcard:

Back of the postcard:

65

Title: *The Castle Corona*

Author: Sharon Creech

Illustrator: David Diaz

Book Overview: First living with an evil master and then moving in with a royal family, orphans Enzio and Pia have a terrific tale for the readers.

Book Distinctions: *Kirkus Reviews* Starred Review

AASL Standards for the 21st-Century Learner Standards: 3.1.3 Write a story using a style like the wordsmith, 4.1.8 Create their story using the illuminated manuscript art style

Content Areas: Language Arts, Art

AR Reading Level: AR: 5.5

Author Web Site: http://www.sharoncreech.com/index.html

Suggested Answers:

1. They discover a pouch left by a thief.

2. The king and his family have forty-seven special assistants. Some of their assistants include: First Dresser, testers, tutor of walking, stable boy, Minister of Defense, Minister of the Daily Schedule, Minister of Meals, Minister of Ceremony, Mistress of Housekeeping, Minister of Village Relations, Ministers of Inventory: Food, Clothing, Horses, Armor, Silver, Gold, Vegetables, Oats, Table Linens

3. Enzio and Pia fear they are being taken to the dungeon because they have the pouch. They are actually brought to be food testers to ensure that the royal family's food is not poisoned.

4. The hermit is their grandfather. They learn that after their parents died, the grandfather made a deal to be the King's hermit as long as the children had a house to stay in and would be brought to the castle when of age.

5. A combination of reader response, creative writing and artwork needed in answer.

The Castle Corona
by Sharon Creech, illustrated by David Diaz

1. What event occurs when Enzio and Pia fetch water for Master Pangini?

2. If you were royalty, what types of assistants would you require? Create a staff list of ten workers for your castle, and compare that to the staff of King Guido and his family.

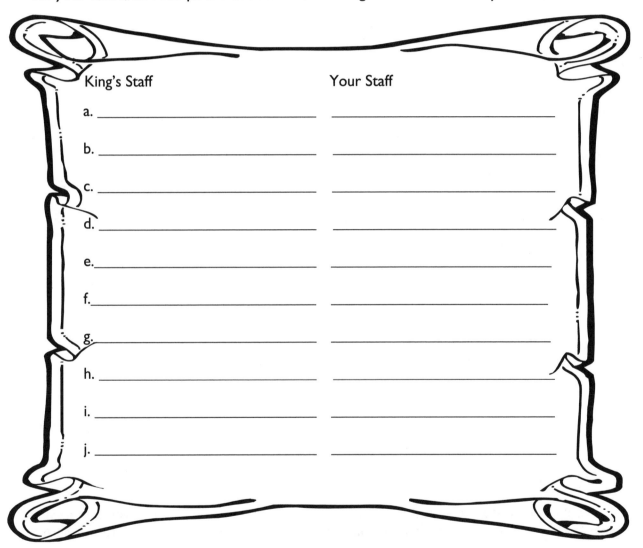

King's Staff   Your Staff

a. _____   _____

b. _____   _____

c. _____   _____

d. _____   _____

e. _____   _____

f. _____   _____

g. _____   _____

h. _____   _____

i. _____   _____

j. _____   _____

3. The King's men take Enzio and Pia. Why do the children think they are being taken? What is the real reason?

4. The King's hermit has a connection to Enzio and Pia. What is that connection?

5. It is now your chance to be a wordsmith. Select four items and characters from the book to start your story. In addition, ask two people to select an item or location for your story.

Character:	Item:
Location:	Additional Item:

Use these items to create a story. On a separate sheet of paper, record your story using the illuminated manuscript art style of David Diaz. Hint: See the first page of each chapter for illustrating ideas.

Title: *The Miraculous Journey of Edward Tulane*

Author: Kate DiCamillo

Illustrator: Bagram Ibatoulline

Book Overview: Superb tale about friendship telling of the travels of an unlikely main character, a three-foot-tall china rabbit.

Book Distinctions: American Library Association 2007 Notable Children's Books, *Publishers Weekly* Starred Review, *School Library Journal* Starred Review, *Kirkus Reviews* Starred Review, *School Library Journal* Best Books 2006, *New York Times* Notable Books 2006, Boston *Globe Horn-Book Award* 2006, Parents' Choice Award 2006, ALA *Booklist* Editors' Choice Books for Youth 2006, Junior Library Guild Selection

AASL Standards for the 21st-Century Learner Standards: 2.1.3 Arrange story events in a graphical organizer

Content Areas: Language Arts, Geography

AR Reading Level: 4.4

Author Web Site: http://www.katedicamillo.com/

Suggested Answers:

1. **Edward Tulane:** They listen to stories together. Edward doesn't like his clothes wrinkled or torn. Martin throws Edward off the boat.

   Susanna: After 279 days on the ocean floor, Edward is caught by a fisherman. Lawrence gives the rabbit as a gift to Nellie. Nellie dresses the rabbit as a girl, but the rabbit does not mind because he loves these people. It is the daughter's act of throwing Edward in the trash during a visit that causes their separation.

   Malone: After 180 days in the garbage, a dog, Lucie, finds Edward and gives him to her master, Bull. Bull is a hobo and dresses Malone as an outlaw. Malone enjoys hearing Bull sing. After being together for nearly seven years, rabbit is flung out of a railcar.

   Clyde: A woman uses Edward to scare crows from her garden. Bryce takes the rabbit down.

   Jangles: Bryce gives Edward as a gift to his ill sister. She rocks him like a baby and likes when he dances. Sadly, they are separated when Sarah dies. Bryce loves making Edward dance as well. He leaves a dangerous situation to go to Memphis. When he doesn't have enough money for dinner, he tries to pay by making the rabbit dance. In the dance, the rabbit smashes to the ground. He seeks the help of Lucius Clarke to help fix the rabbit, but because he does not have the money to pay for the repair, the rabbit now belongs to Lucius. Bryce is not allowed to visit the store to see the rabbit again.

   He: A positive aspect, if there is one at this point in the book, is that Edward is around other toys. Nearly five years later, a young girl convinces her mother to purchase him.

   Edward: Maggie is Abilene's daughter. Prediction of memories and separation are reader response.

2. Answer is reader response but students need to be able to defend their selection.

The Miraculous Journey of Edward Tulane
by Kate DiCamillo, illustrated by Bagram Ibatoulline

1. Edward's journey allows him to meet many new people. Each person wants a china rabbit for a different reason, and often each has his or her own idea about what Edward should be named. Create a chart like the following with plenty of room for writing your answers. Next to the rabbit's names and the owner's information, write down memories the owner shared with the rabbit. In the last column, write how Edward and the owner were separated.

Rabbit's Names	Owner & Location	Memories	Cause of Separation
Edward Tulane	Abilene Tulane Egypt Street		
Susanna	Nellie and Lawrence Fishing town		
Malone	Bull and Lucy Traveling		
Clyde	Gardening woman Garden		
Jangles	Sarah Ruth House		
	Bryce Memphis		
He	Lucius Clarke Toy store		
Edward	Maggie Toy store	Predict…	Predict…

2. If Edward had to choose his favorite owner, whom do you think he would select? Why?

From *Active Reading: Activities for Librarians and Teachers* by Beth McGuire.
Westport, CT: Libraries Unlimited. Copyright © 2009.

Title: *Vanishing Act: Mystery at the U.S. Open*

Author: John Feinstein

Book Overview: A realistic sport fiction book that takes the reader on one adventure to solve another, with main character Stevie and Carol during a precarious situation.

Book Distinctions: Junior Library Guild Selection

AASL Standards for the 21st-Century Learner Standards: 1.1.4 Locate and assess sources, 3.1.3 Write a factual story suitable for newspaper publication

Content Areas: Physical Education, Language Arts

AR Reading Level: 4.8

Suggested Answers:

1. College basketball

2. There is a kidnapping.

3. He is an agent.

4. Reader response

5. Reader response

Vanishing Act: Mystery at the U.S. Open
by John Feinstein

Answer the following questions.

1. Stevie and Carol are off for another writing adventure shortly after covering what sporting event?

   _____

   _____

   _____

2. What front-page news occurs when they are at the U.S. Open?

   _____

   _____

   _____

3. What interest does Carol's uncle have in sports?

   _____

   _____

   _____

4. What sporting event would you like to report about the most?

   _____

   _____

   _____

5. Think of another sporting event that Stevie and Carol could follow. Create a shocking lead.

   _____

   _____

   _____

All good reporters make sure to know the background of the event they are covering. How would you provide a written overview of the U.S. Open in two paragraphs while summarizing the plot of the book and remaining creative? Try it now on the back of this sheet! Don't forget to cover who, what, why, where and when of the U.S. Open. Use print sources and www.usopen.org.

Title: *The Entertainer and the Dybbuk*

Author: Sid Fleischman

Book Overview: This historical fiction novel presents a unique way for readers to learn more about the hardships people endured during World War II.

Book Distinctions: Sydney Taylor Award, older readers category, *Kirkus Reviews* Starred Review, *School Library Journal* starred review, Junior Library Guild Selection

AASL Standards for the 21st-Century Learner Standards: 1.1.4 Locate and assess sources, 4.1.8 Create a storyboard for a skit based on the information presented in the novel

Content Areas: History, Language Arts

AR Reading Level: 3.7

Author Web Site: http://www.sidfleischman.com/

Suggested Answers:

1. He is seeking fame.

2. He is a boy who died before he was thirteen years old. He saved Freddie's life during the war and now would like Freddie to help him finish the goals he never achieved.

3. Not well. The routine is cancelled.

4. It is a spirit.

5. He talks even when Freddie drinks or has his lips taped.

6. Reader response.

7. He wants to have a bar mitzvah.

8. Polly is his ex-girlfriend, but they are now hanging out together. She thinks that he is lying about not revealing his Jewish faith to her.

9. He is the worst child killer during World War II. He has a fake tattoo to avoid being identified. They learn his location from a dealer.

10. Avrom makes the officer confess.

11. Reader response based on facts.

The Entertainer and the Dybbuk
by Sid Fleischman

1. What is Freddie doing in Austria three years after World War II?

2. Who is Avrom Amos Poliakov?

3. How is the Count Dracula routine received by the public?

4. What is a dybbuk?

5. How does the dybbuk help Freddie with his act?

6. What would you suggest Freddie do to add humor to his Count Dracula routine?

7. What is the first major goal that Avrom wants Freddie to help him achieve?

8. Who is Polly, and what does she think Freddie is lying about?

9. Who is SS Colonel Gerhard Junker-Strupp? How do they learn his whereabouts?

10. Avrom and Freddie are present at the trial. What causes the defendant to be found guilty?

11. This novel is based on historical events. What facts can you abstract from the novel? Select one fact and conduct research from multiple sources. Create a skit story board below that would be suitable for Freddie. Use another sheet of paper if you prefer.

Title: *Football Genius: A Novel*

Author: Tim Green

Book Overview: Having a chance to visit the field during a National Football League game is just the beginning of the excitement for Troy and his life's happiness. This book is written with sport realism by a former NFL player.

AASL Standards for the 21st-Century Learner Standards: 4.1.2 Reflect upon book events and compare to personal reactions

Content Areas: Language Arts, Physical Education

AR Reading Level: 4.8

Author Web Site: http://www.timgreenbooks.com/

Suggested Answers:

1. Seth calls him that when watching the Georgia Tech game together because Troy calls the plays correctly.

2. Reader response.

3. Jamie's dad is the coach and can't see past the family connection.

4. Troy's mother has a public relations job with the Atlanta Falcons. Reader response.

5. Tate wins a contest and pretends to get sick. The real goal was to play matchmaker.

6. Yes. For example, he tipped Seth to the play, and the ball ended up being intercepted by the Falcons.

7. Reader response.

Football Genius: A Novel
by Tim Green

1. How does Troy get the nickname "Football Genius"? Who gives him the name?

2. Troy has two good friends: Tate and Nathan. Which friend would you like to visit with? Why?

3. Jamie is the starting quarterback, and Troy is second string. What is the reason for the lineup?

4. Where does Troy's mom get a job? Would you be interested in a job like that?

5. How does Seth and Troy's mom end up together for lunch?

6. Does Troy prove to be helpful from the sidelines? Support your response.

7. Do you think Troy will continue being a "Football Genius"? Explain.

From *Active Reading: Activities for Librarians and Teachers* by Beth McGuire.
Westport, CT: Libraries Unlimited. Copyright © 2009.

Title: *The Silver Donkey*

Author: Sonya Hartnett

Illustrator: Don Powers

Book Overview: As a soldier attempts to return home, he shares stories from the war with the young children who are trying to nurse him back to health despite the gravity of the soldier's situation.

Book Distinctions: *Publishers Weekly* Starred Review, Children's Book of the Year Award 2005 (Children's Book Council of Australia), Junior Library Guild Selection

AASL Standards for the 21st-Century Learner Standards: 1.1.4 Locate and assess sources, 2.1.3 Analyze information and apply current day situations and personal reactions to events

Content Area: Language Arts

AR Reading Level: 5.0

Suggested Answers:

1. They find Lieutenant Shepard.

2. He has a silver donkey charm.

3. It was a gift from his sick brother.

4. Reader response.

5. Reader response.

6. Reader response.

7. Answers will vary but must be supported by facts.

The Silver Donkey
by Sonya Hartnett, illustrated by Don Powers

1. One day the children find a person in the forest. Who do they find?

2. What possession does he have with him?

3. What is the significance of the item?

4. The children secretly visit the soldier in the forest and anticipate his stories. Pascal is disappointed not to hear about war, but on reflection he sees that war is not glorious, nor is it fun. If a friend or family member of yours were sent to war, what item would you give that person? What would that item represent?

5. If you were sent to war, what item would you want to take with you?

6. Visit databases and view military documents regarding WWI. What information have you learned? Read three sources.

7. Does war look like something to be taken lightly? Why? Use facts to support your claim.

From *Active Reading: Activities for Librarians and Teachers* by Beth McGuire. Westport, CT: Libraries Unlimited. Copyright © 2009.

Title: *George's Secret Key to the Universe*

Authors: Lucy and Stephen Hawking. With Christophe Galfard, Ph.D.

Illustrator: Garry Parsons

Book Overview: Put together progressive scientific minds and a breathtaking futuristic space exploration paired with NASA photography and current resource, and you have a rare and fine read.

Book Distinctions: *Publishers Weekly* Starred Review, the *Today Show*'s Al's Book Club for Kids

AASL Standards for the 21st-Century Learner Standards: 3.1.3 Demonstrate an understanding of the topics in both writing and speaking, 3.1.6 Use book and online information properly

Content Areas: Science, Mathematics, Language Arts

AR Reading Level: 5.6

Book-Related Web Site: http://www.secretkeytotheuniverse.com/

Suggested Answers:

1. Although answers will vary, Annie's family has a talking computer named Cosmos and George's family strives for a simple life without a computer.

2. Riding a comet to Saturn. They gaze at Jupiter when an asteroid storm occurs. Students' choices are opinion based on facts from the book.

3. The temperatures from the book in order:

    –454.72 F: average space temperature

    –240 F: average Moon night temperature

    –128.2 F: lowest temperature on Earth

    59 F: average temperature on Earth

    136.4 F: hottest temperature on Earth

    230 F: average day temperature on the Moon

    9,932 F: average surface temperature of the Sun

    27,000,000 F: average temperature of the Sun core

Student responses for high and low earth temperatures will vary. A great Web site tool to make a graph can be found at The Kids' Zone section of the National Center for Educational Statistics: http://nces.ed.gov/nceskids/createagraph/. The monthly high and low temperatures can be found at *USA Today* online: http://www.usatoday.com/weather/wext.htm

4. George wants to win the computer prize.

5. They used to work together but had different views. Reeper was seen as dangerous.

6. Answers will be based on facts gathered.

George's Secret Key to the Universe by Lucy and Stephen Hawking. With Christophe Galfard, Ph.D., illustrated by Garry Parsons

1. George thinks he meets a parent different from his own when he meets Annie's father Eric, but as they begin talking, Annie thinks George's parents are very curious. Compare George's, Annie's, and your family using the chart below.

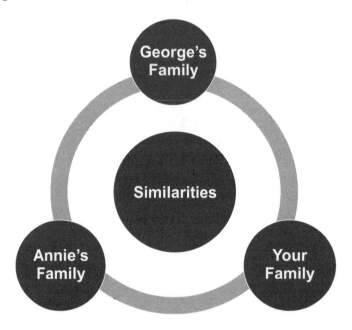

2. Annie takes George on a special trip. Where do they visit? Which place would you most like to visit? What would you learn?

3. What was the hottest day in your town last month? How about the coldest day last month?

   Check weather statistics and find the warmest and coldest days last month.

   The hottest day last month: _____

   The coldest day last month: _____

   Take those temperatures along with the temperatures shared on page 79 of the novel to create a temperature chart. Arrange your chart from lowest to highest temperatures. Draw the chart by hand, or create it using a technology application. Your chart will have ten different temperatures.

4. Why is George so intent on signing up for the science competition?

5. Eric and Dr. Reeper know each other. How do they know each other, and what caused their friendship to deteriorate? Do you think that their friendship will be rejuvenated? Why or why not?

6. Select one of the photographs from Cosmos's Picture Files in the novel. Research additional facts about the size of the location, the composition and facts you find intriguing on the topic and prepare a brief presentation to the class. Options include: Earth's moon, Horsehead Nebula, Pillars of Creation, Milky Way, Sun, Proxima Centauri, Eta Carinae, Helix Nebula, Hyakutake, Halley's Comet, Comet SWAN, Deep Impact Spacecraft, Saturn, Titan, Rhea, Iapetus, Dione, Tethys, Enceladus, Jupiter, Io, Europa, Ganymede, Callisto, Mars, Phobos, Deimos, Ceres, Pluto, Eris, Andromeda galaxy, exoosolar planet, NGC 4261, NGC 7052, M87, and Earth. Take notes on an additional piece of paper if needed.

Topic	
Size	
Location	
Intriguing facts	
Resources	

Title: *Toby Wheeler: Eighth-Grade Benchwarmer*

Author: Thatcher Heldring

Book Overview: Playing recreation basketball is a source of enjoyment for Toby, but playing for his middle school team proves to be more difficult as his best friend becomes more distant, and Toby becomes friends with the strict coach's daughter, who plays a better game of basketball than he does.

Book Distinctions: Junior Library Guild Selection

AASL Standards for the 21st-Century Learner Standards: 4.1.7 Use appropriate tools to write and produce a sport segment based on the text

Content Areas: Language Arts, Physical Education

AR Reading Level: 4.2

Author Web Site: http://thatchertheauthor.com/

Suggested Answers:

1. JJ

2. No, JJ plays in a band with Stephen and spends lots of time with Valerie. He would rather use spending time with Toby as an alibi.

3. Megan plays on Toby's team. The record shared is 8,497,330 to 1. This would seem to be an exaggeration.

4. Toby tutors her in math, and she tutors him in basketball.

5. He writes a note to reinforce that they can just be friends, which makes her think he is choosing basketball over her.

6. He learns it is not bad to be a benchwarmer or "pinerider."

7. Readers response.

Toby Wheeler: Eighth-Grade Benchwarmer
by Thatcher Heldring

1. Who is one of Toby's best friends at the start of the novel?

2. Do they remain best friends? Explain your answer.

3. How does Toby beat Vinny in a basketball game? What win-loss record is shared with the reader? Do you think that it is correct?

4. Toby is assigned to help Megan with a skill, and later she is assigned to tutor Toby. In what skill do they tutor each other? Are each successful? Explain?

5. Why does Toby give Megan a note?

6. Megan introduces Toby to Old Dude. What does Toby learn from him?

7. Create a sport segment suitable for a news station about the basketball season at Toby's school. Be sure to include information about the teammates, coach, records, opponents, and school. Write your segment on the back of this sheet and then create your audiovisual presentation with the technology and equipment available.

From *Active Reading: Activities for Librarians and Teachers* by Beth McGuire.
Westport, CT: Libraries Unlimited. Copyright © 2009.

Title: *Middle School Is Worse than Meatloaf: A Year Told through Stuff*

Author: Jennifer L. Holm

Illustrations: Elicia Castaldi

Book Overview: Reading another individual's diary provides insight, and reading through their personal stuff opens numerous doors, providing an insider's look into the main character's year in middle school.

Book Distinctions: New York Public Library 100 Titles for Reading and Sharing 2007, National Parenting Publication Award, Gold Award, *Publishers Weekly* Starred Review, Junior Library Guild Selection, Book Sense Children's Picks, Fall 2007

AASL Standards for the 21st-Century Learner Standards: 4.1.7 Use social networking applications to create a scrapbook page

Content Area: Language Arts

AR Reading Level: 4.7

Author Web Site: http://www.jenniferholm.com/

Suggested Answers:

1. Character descriptions can vary but should be similar.

   Brian: Asks Ginny to the Spring Fling.

   Henry: Gets into a lot of trouble for dropping cherry bombs in the school toilet, among other things, and is sent to a military academy.

   Timmy: Enrolled in kindergarten and has the role of a donkey in the Christmas pageant.

   Mary Catherine: She has been Ginny's best friend since kindergarten until Ginny got a role in Swan Lake last year. She still has not returned Ginny's pink sweater.

   Becky Soo: Ginny's friend who is taking horseback riding lessons.

2. Activity. After registering for a free account at www.smilebox.com, students can create a scrapbook page.

3. Reader response. Online applications including Glogstar (http://www.glogster.com/) and Flicker (http://www.flickr.com) can provide a great framework for a collage. Students will need to create a free account to create a collage. Be sure to stress to the students the importance of Web safety, privacy, and secure posting.

4. Presentation

Middle School Is Worse than Meatloaf: A Year Told through Stuff
by Jennifer L. Holm, pictures by Elicia Castaldi

Ginny's year is told through a variety of items, including her to-do list, schedule, receipts, notes, newspaper clippings, assignments, and postcards.

1. Give a brief description of each of the following characters. Locate a clipping from a magazine or newspaper that reminds you of each character, and then paste them together to make a collage. Affix the character's name to the appropriate section.

Brian:
Henry:
Timmy:
Mary Catherine:
Becky Soo:

2. Make a prediction for Ginny's summer. Create a collage. Use the old-fashioned cut-and-paste method or an online application. Paste your collage below.

3. Create a scrapbook page based on your year so far on another piece of paper, or using other tools that your teacher suggests.

4. Share the scrapbook page with the class.

Title: *Cracker!: The Best Dog in Vietnam*

Author: Cynthia Kadohata

Book Overview: Visit Vietnam through the soldiers, trained dogs, and the general public in a compelling historical fiction novel.

Book Distinctions: ALA *Booklist* Starred Review, *Book Sense* Children's Picks Spring 2007, Junior Library Guild Selection

AASL Standards for the 21st-Century Learner Standards: 3.1.3 Write a story incorporating realities from Vietnam

Content Areas: Language Arts, History

AR Reading Level: 4.9

Author Web Site: http://www.kira-kira.us/

Suggested Answers:

1. Dogs are not permitted in their new apartment.

2. He is not sure that he wants to work in his father's hardware store because he finds it dull at times, and in his mind, he is a man ready for responsibility and to "whip the world."

3. The dogs smell out traps navigating soldiers through hot zones. Nearly 150 men are led by Rick and Cracker.

4. Creative response supported with facts and material from the novel.

Cracker!: The Best Dog in Vietnam
by Cynthia Kadohata

1. What is the main reason that Willie's parents have to get rid of his beloved dog, Cracker?

2. What reasons cause Rick Hanski to enlist in the U.S. Army at seventeen years old?

3. How do Cracker and other dogs help the American effort in Vietnam?

4. The author provides insight into how Cracker thinks in a variety of situations. We also learn how Willie feels about his dog, and Rick writes letter after letter trying to save Cracker. The military officially views dogs as objects. Think about other objects in the novel. Examples are E-tool, c-rat, sandbags, APC, poncho, stretcher, and plane. If these objects could write a letter, what would they write about? Focus on one of the objects. Write a letter from the viewpoint of that object, based on the situations you read about in the novel. The letter can include the soldiers who used the object, the locations where the object was, the ways it was used, and the events it witnessed. Write your final letter in the shape of the object you chose.

From *Active Reading: Activities for Librarians and Teachers* by Beth McGuire.
Westport, CT: Libraries Unlimited. Copyright © 2009.

Title: *Magpie Gabbard and the Quest for the Buried Moon*

Author: Sally M. Keehn

Book Overview: Put together goblins, visions from a kettle, a family feud, and a goal to save the moon, and there is a story to share.

Book Distinctions: *Publishers Weekly* Starred Review, Junior Library Guild Selection

AASL Standards for the 21st-Century Learner Standards: 3.1.3 Compose a thank you note based on the kindness the moon exhibits

Content Area: Language Arts

AR Reading Level: 4.4

Author Web Site: http://www.sallykeehn.com/

Suggested Answers:

1. She wants to see her brother, Milo, and give him his foot.

2. One reason is that Grandpa lost the sheriff election by thirty votes, which are thought to be the 30 Sizemores who did not vote for him as promised.

3. Thelma put too much Bug Dirt on the Horn Heard that she made for Randall, and he gets sick. Daddy needs to fetch more Green Water to help save Randall, but he is bit by a goblin.

4. The families work together.

5. Reader response. Final copies can be created from construction paper or produced with Internet or computer resources.

Magpie Gabbard and the Quest for the Buried Moon
by Sally M. Keehn

1. What do you hope to do or receive as a gift for your thirteenth birthday? Is this similar to Magpie's thirteenth birthday wishes? Why or why not?

2. What is one reason for the Gabbard and Sizemore feud? Answers can be found in regard to the Sorrow Chain.

3. What happens to Randall and her dad that leaves Magpie in charge?

4. How do they get the moon back?

5. Write a thank you note from the moon to Magpie. Create a final copy that Magpie could deliver to the moon.

Title: *Me and the Pumpkin Queen*

Author: Marlane Kennedy

Book Overview: Mildred's mother was the Pumpkin Queen when she was in eleventh grade, but now it is Mildred's turn to try and shine as she strives for first place in the pumpkin contest.

Book Distinctions: Book Sense Children's Picks Fall 2007, Junior Library Guild Selection

AASL Standards for the 21st-Century Learner Standards: 1.1.4 Locate, assess, and summarize information from Web sites

Content Areas: Science, Language Arts

AR Reading Level: 4.8

Author Web Site: http://www.marlanekennedy.com/

Suggested Answers:

1. When she is six years old and at the pumpkin show for the first time without her mother, her interest blossoms.

2. She wants to take her shopping for clothes. Mildred would rather spend time reading about pumpkins.

3. She selects Howard Dill. He shared his pumpkin success freely instead of patenting his seeds. Earning money was not his goal. The remainder of the question is reader response.

4. Very well. She wins the pumpkin competition.

5. She gives him seeds from her prize pumpkin even though he was a sore loser. The rest of the answer is an opinion.

6. The Web site mentioned in the book is www.bigpumpkin.com. Individual notes will vary.

Me and the Pumpkin Queen
by Marlane Kennedy

1. How does Mildred get interested in pumpkin growing?

2. Where does her aunt want to take Mildred? Is Mildred excited? Explain.

3. One of Mildred's class projects is to write a paper on someone whom she has never met but inspires her. Who does Mildred choose to write about? Do you think this person is inspiring? Why?

    Which person would you select? Explain your choice.

4. How does the pumpkin competition go for Mildred?

5. What does Mildred give Grover Fernart at the end of the novel? How do you think Grover reacted once Mildred was out of sight?

6. Web activity: Mildred likes a specific Web site. What is the Web address?

    Pretend that you are taking notes for Mildred when she is out shopping with her aunt and can't visit the Web site for information. Write her notes.

    Surprise Mildred with a new Web site filled with solid information about pumpkins. Provide the site address below and a helpful feature from the site.

Web Site: **Helpful Feature:**

From *Active Reading: Activities for Librarians and Teachers* by Beth McGuire.
Westport, CT: Libraries Unlimited. Copyright © 2009.

Title: *Diary of a Wimpy Kid*

Author: Jeff Kinney

Book Overview: Being in middle school is difficult enough without having a little brother who is a perfect angel in his parents' eyes and an older brother with a wild band and a crazy student council election underway.

Book Distinctions: New York Public Library 100 Titles for Reading and Sharing 2007, National Parenting Publication Award, Gold Award, *Publishers Weekly* Review Starred Review, *Publishers Weekly* Best Children's Books of 2007, Junior Library Guild Selection, *Book Sense* Children's Picks Winter 2007/2008, Quill Children's Chapter/Middle Grade Award Nominee

AASL Standards for the 21st-Century Learner Standards: 4.1.8 Create a comic based on the book content

Content Area: Language Arts

AR Reading Level: 5.2

Author Web Site: http://www.wimpykid.com/

Suggested Answers:

Rodrick: brother, has a band

Manny: little brother, does no wrong in parents' eyes

Rowley: best friend, class clown

Principal: tears slanderous posters down

Teacher: edits comic

Student-created comics will vary. One Web-based resource to create comics is http://www.comeeko.com. After opening a free account, students can create personalized comic strips.

Diary of a Wimpy Kid by Jeff Kinney

Design a comic suitable to place in the school paper that would summarize the book *Diary of a Wimpy Kid*. To help you get started, write brief descriptions to describe the following people in the book.

Roderick	Manny
Rowley	**Principal**
Teacher	**You**

You can create your comic on construction paper, using a computer program, or with Web-based software suggested by your teacher.

From *Active Reading: Activities for Librarians and Teachers* by Beth McGuire.
Westport, CT: Libraries Unlimited. Copyright © 2009.

Title: *The Book of Story Beginnings*

Author: Kristin Kladstrup

Book Overview: Imagine writing a story only to find yourself living in the fictional setting you created, and your family assumes you ran away. How could you return?

Book Distinctions: Junior Library Guild Selection

AASL Standards for the 21st-Century Learner Standards: 4.1.2 Reflect on character choices compared with students' own

Content Area: Language Arts

AR Reading Level: 4.5

Suggested Answers:

1. Her dad did not get tenure, and Aunt Lavonne leaves her house to them in her will.

2. One month after his disappearance, a rowboat was found in the lawn. They do not live near a body of water.

3. Reader response.

4. Students write their own story beginning.

5. Student opinion supported by character information from the book.

6. Oscar decides to stay in the present even though it is believed that the traveling talisman will work. He makes this decision for several reasons, one of which is that his arrival in the past could change the present. For example, after high school, he planned to travel with his best friend, Earl. Instead, Earl went to college, and he might not have if Oscar stayed in the past. Student opinion as to what they would do if in Oscar's situation.

The Book of Story Beginnings
by Kristin Kladstrup

1. Why is Lucy's family moving to Iowa?

2. Explain the mysterious disappearance of Oscar back in 1914.

3. If you found the book in which Lucy and Oscar wrote their story beginnings, would you try writing a story beginning in the book as well? Why or why not?

4. Try writing your very own story below. You be the judge if the start needs to be erased.

5. Which character from the novel would you most like to have as a guest speaker at your school? Why did you make your choice?

6. Oscar has a choice to remain in the present or try to go back to the past. What does he decide to do? Why? Would you have made the same decision if you were in his shoes?

Title: *The Mysterious Edge of the Heroic World*

Author: E. L. Konigsburg

Book Overview: The artwork of the past ties families of the present to events that changed the course of history.

Book Distinctions: Book Sense Children's Picks Winter 2007/2008, Junior Library Guild Selection

AASL Standards for the 21st-Century Learner Standards: 1.1.1 Students conduct inquiry to expand knowledge while selecting and defending their choice

Content Areas: Language Arts, History, Art

AR Reading Level: 5.7

Suggested Answers:

1. St. Malo, Florida

2. He took one silk-screen photo that his mom thought was valuable, but no one else agreed, to the Smithsonian. The museum eventually purchased it for $20,000.

3. They help prepare for the liquidation of her items as she nears her move to a retirement community.

4. Amedeo's godfather. He is intelligent and focused on work; he is losing his hair, in his twenties, and loves research.

5. She gives him a box containing stories of his father's life.

6. Reader response.

7. Hitler was twice denied admission into the Vienna Art Academy, which is thought to have caused his disdain for modern art. Hitler believed that artwork should depict nature. According to the novel, more than 16,000 pieces of "degenerate" artwork were stolen under Hitler's orders; 650 pieces were put on display as degenerate art to highlight what he considered evil.

8. Aida Lily Tull loved singing and had a well-received operatic voice. While in Europe, she met her husband and became Mrs. Zender.

9. Up for sale at $5,000 is *The Moon Lady* drawing by Modigliani. Amedeo thinks the price is too low, and he tells the buyers that Mrs. Zender has withdrawn the piece. In actuality, she did not. In talking with his godfather, they realize that the box is linked to the artwork. They learn that Eisenhuth gave Mr. Zender the artwork to woo a widow, but the widow was Lily's mom and wanted Lily to be with him. He kept Eisenhuth's Nazi past a secret.

10. Sheboygan Art Center, Wisconsin. It is a gift of John and Lelani in memory of Pieter van der Waal.

11. This response is a combination of reader response, inference, and research.

The Mysterious Edge of the Heroic World
by E. L. Konigsburg

1. Where does Amedeo Kaplan move?

2. How did William Wilcox help his mother with a silk screen?

3. What do Amedeo and William do at Mrs. Zender's house?

4. Who is Peter Vanderwaal? Describe his personality.

5. What does Peter's mom give him? What is found in the item?

6. William gives Amedeo twenty-four seconds to list the talents he has. Take twenty-four seconds to think of your talents and write them below.

7. How did Hitler feel about artwork? What did he do with degenerate art?

8. What is Mrs. Zender's history? Where did she live? What did she do for her livelihood?

9. What is the story of The Moon Lady?

10. Where is The Moon Lady at the end of the book?

11. The works of Henri Matisse, Pierre-Auguste Renoir, Pablo Picasso, Vincent van Gogh, Marc Chagall, and Georges Braque are featured in Peter's gala. Select an artist to research using various resources. Explain why their art is ideal for the gala.

Title: *Schooled*

Author: Gordon Korman

Book Overview: The first day at a new school tends to be shocking and is certainly so when it is your first day in the eighth grade and at public school.

Book Distinctions: ALA *Booklist* Starred Review

AASL Standards for the 21st-Century Learner Standards: 3.1.5 Students apply charity research to needs of their community

Content Area: Language Arts

AR Reading Level: 4.9

Author Web Site: http://gordonkorman.com

Suggested Answers:

1. Capricorn and Rain live there.

2. Zach thinks he has picked the perfect candidate for class president. It is a school tradition to pick a social outcast and watch a class president fail. Hugh would have most likely ended up as president if Cap did not enter their school.

3. Cap is only thirteen years old. A. Getting Rain to the hospital. B. Getting the bus driver to the hospital. C. Helping Sophie learn to drive.

4. He has spitballs launched at him, and a dead bird and fake love notes placed in his locker. He is even tricked into wearing the jersey of the rival team during a pep rally and gets tackled. Cap does not resort to violence, but the manner of his handling things will extend into reader opinion.

5. March of Caring—$1,000.00

   Food Drive—$800.00

   Cancer Research—$500.00

   Alzheimer's Disease—$500.00

   March of Dimes—$650

   Reader response for the charity fundraiser.

6. Answers could include the increased interest in art and the tie-dye activity. Also more students had more activity learning his tai chi routine. In addition, a record number of students volunteered for the dance.

7. Rain changes her style to the contemporary. She sells the commune for $17 million and purchases a condo in the district of Claverage Middle School. Readers give their opinion as to whether this is shocking and why or why not.

Schooled by Gordon Korman

1. Who lives at the Garland Alternative Farm Commune?

2. Both Hugh and Zach are initially pleased with Cap's arrival to their school, but for different reasons. Explain.

3. Why is it odd that Cap knows how to drive?

   Give three different situations in which Cap's driving skills helped.

   A.

   B.

   C.

4. Some students at school are cruel and bully Cap. What happens? Does Cap handle the situations well?

5. How much money does Cap donate with the Claverage Middle School Student Activity Fund to the following charities?

Charity	Amount
March of Caring	
Food Drive	
Cancer Research	
Alzheimer's Disease	
March of Dimes	

   Research charities in your community and decide which you would like to suggest to your student council or class president as a good one to organize a fundraiser for.

6. Pinpoint two examples of positive school change as a result of Cap's leadership and interest to learn the names of all 1,000-plus students.

7. What does Rain do at the end of the novel? Does this surprise you? Why or why not?

From *Active Reading: Activities for Librarians and Teachers* by Beth McGuire. Westport, CT: Libraries Unlimited. Copyright © 2009.

Title: *Theodosia and the Serpents of Chaos*

Author: R. L. LaFevers

Illustrator: Yoko Tanaka

Book Overview: Searching for treasure, displaying artifacts, and performing magic take the reader along on a perilous journey.

Book Distinctions: *Publishers Weekly* Starred Review, ALA *Booklist* Starred Review, Book Sense Children's Picks Summer 2007, Junior Library Guild Selection

AASL Standards for the 21st-Century Learner Standards: 2.1.6 Create a travel brochure based on research, 3.1.6 Provide source citations

Content Areas: Geography, History, Language Arts

AR Reading Level: 5.2

Author Web Site: http://www.rllafevers.com/about.html

Suggested Answers:

1. Her dad is the head curator there.

2. Her talent is a secret. She can locate the black magic on items and remove it.

3. It is the heart of Egypt from Amenemhab's Tomb.

4. He tells her that she is being followed.

5. Individual topics and brochures will vary. Brochures can be made with construction paper. Another option is for students to use computer applications such as Microsoft Publisher or Web-based products.

Theodosia and the Serpents of Chaos
by R. L. LaFevers, illustrated by Yoko Tanaka

1. Why does Theodosia (Theo) spend so much time in the Museum of Legends and Antiques?

2. Theo has a special talent. What is it?

3. When Theo's mother arrives, she tells of a wonderful item she has found. What did she find?

4. Sticky Will, a street urchin, helps Theo a lot. How does he help?

5. When in Egypt: Choose one of the selections below and conduct research. Make a tourist brochure. Be sure to cite your sources.

   - Antony and Cleopatra
   - Lighthouse of Pharos
   - Library of Alexandria
   - Valley of Kings

Title: *Missing Magic*

Author: Emma Laybourn

Book Overview: Try attending a school with students who all have the skills to perform magic—except you.

Book Distinctions: Junior Library Guild Selection

AASL Standards for the 21st-Century Learner Standards: 4.1.5 Relate personal interests and strengths to create a lesson

Content Areas: Language Arts

AR Reading Level: 4.3

Suggested Answers:

1. His famous Uncle Kelver pays for him.

2. She has the ability to see parts of the future.

3. Kidnapping students.

4. Ned is spared because his uncle is famous.

5. She uses her magic to transform into a mermaid and distract the crew. Kelver takes her magic away.

6. Reader response.

Missing Magic by Emma Laybourn

1. Although Ned has no magic, he is attending a school for magical students. How and why he is at this school?

2. Cassie has a magic skill that she would rather not possess. What is her skill?

3. The Necromancers are causing a great deal of fear. What are the Necromancers doing?

4. Why doesn't Lady Galera throw Ned overboard?

5. Cassie puts herself in great peril. What does she do, and what is the result of her efforts?

6. Ned is accepting applications for teachers to give a lesson without magic. Applicants need to send a written plan and a video overview to be considered. If you were applying for the job, what would you like to teach? What would you call your lesson to get the students excited? How long would your lesson be? Would you assign homework? Make a plan on the back of this page and create a video sample of your lesson if time allows.

Title: *Fairest*

Author: Gail Carson Levine

Book Overview: Does the quality of fairest rest more in image or action?

Book Distinctions: *Publishers Weekly* Starred Review, *School Library Journal* Starred Review, ALA *Booklist* Starred Review, ALA *Booklist* Editors' Choice Books for Youth 2006, *School Library Journal* Best Books 2006, Junior Library Guild Selection

AASL Standards for the 21st-Century Learner Standards: 4.1.8 Students create a song comparing their lives to Aza's and record it using available technology

Content Areas: Language Arts

Activity Skills: recall, comparison, evaluation, create a song, record the song using available technology

AR Reading Level: 4.1

Suggested Answers:

1. Its singers.

2. Never.

3. She asks Aza to be a lady in waiting.

4. Her family will get fifty acres of land. The family would not have had enough money to purchase such a large amount of land.

5. Reader response.

6. Reader response; song is to be recorded.

1. What is Aza's land famous for?

2. What response does the gnome give Aza when she asks if she will be beautiful one day?

3. The queen asks Aza to serve a role. What is that role?

4. Aza's family will benefit from this new role. What will they receive? How will this help her family?

5. Is Ivy a good queen? Why?

6. Write a song at least four lines long that you would like to sing. This song is to compare your life with Aza's. Record your song using available technology and share it with the class.

Title: *Gossamer*

Author: Lois Lowry

Book Overview: Ever wonder how where a good dream or a nightmare comes from?

Book Distinctions: American Library Association 2007 Notable Children's Books, Parents' Choice Award 2006, ALA *Booklist* Starred Review, *Publishers Weekly* Starred Review, *School Library Journal* Starred Review, Junior Library Guild Selection

AASL Standards for the 21st-Century Learner Standards: 3.1.6 Use book and online information properly

Content Areas: Language Arts, Psychology

AR Reading Level: 4.4

Author Web Site: http://www.loislowry.com/

Suggested Answers:

1. He thinks she is too curious.

2. Dream-givers touch items in the house.

3. John. His dad was cruel and abusive, and also abused his mother. She was very intimidated by him. John has lived with a different family, but they "returned him." John's mother is working hard so that she can get John back. Yes, they are successful bestowing happy dreams. They are so successful that an entire horde of sinisteeds visit to inflict nightmares.

4. Reader response.

5. Reader response.

Gossamer by Lois Lowry

1. Why does Fastidious not want to train Littlest?

2. How do dream-givers know what to share in dreams?

3. One woman whom they visit begins to look after a young boy. What is his name? It becomes a challenge to bestow happy moments to the boy. Why is this the case? Are Thin Elderly and Littlest successful? Explain.

4. If Littlest visited you, what items would help her complete the job? What would your favorite dream be?

5. Have you ever remembered some of your dreams when you wake in the morning? Look up different types of dreams in a dream dictionary (found in your library). Use the dictionary to make interpretations of your dreams since you don't have Gossamer to help you. List them below.

Title: *What-the-Dickens: The Story of a Rogue Tooth Fairy*

Author: Gregory Maguire

Book Overview: Readers find answers as to how their teeth are taken and coins are left in their place, in addition to the history and goal of the skibbereen.

AASL Standards for the 21st-Century Learner Standards: 4.1.8 Create a drawing of a tooth fairy based on the description of the book

Content Areas: Language Arts, Psychology

AR Reading Level: 5

Author Web Site: http://www.gregorymaguire.com/children/

Suggested Answers:

1. When an orphan sees him in a can, his first response is "What the dickens —?"

2. He pulls a tiger tooth out at the zoo and presents it to McCavity. This plan is unsuccessful.

3. She spends a good deal of time explaining their job instead of working. She is a few moments late with the tooth and receives demerits.

4. The tooth fairy is a silly girl dancing in the sky with a flying toothbrush called Tickles. Actual drawings will differ.

5. Agents of Change: They travel alone and make the tooth trade possible.

   Wish Team: They deliver dreams.

   Laborers: These include the Scavengers, who collect money, and the Harvesters, who plant the teeth.

6. Reader response.

What-the-Dickens: The Story of a Rogue Tooth Fairy
by Gregory Maguire

1. How does the skibbereen get the name "What-the-Dickens"?

2. What-the-Dickens wants to impress the cat McCavity. What does the skibbereen do to try to impress the cat? Does it work?

A wisdom tooth.

3. When What-the-Dickens originally meets Pepper, does he help her on the tooth mission? Explain.

4. During the parade, the first illustration of a tooth fairy is shared. Write a sentence to describe their appearance. Then draw a sketch of the tooth fairy based on the information provided.

5. What job descriptions for the skibbereen are found in the book? Which job would you be best suited for?

6. Gage learns about their colony. Do you think that Dinah will ever find Pepper or What-the-Dickens? Come up with a plan to help Dinah make their meeting happen, and write it here.

Title: *Jeremy Fink and the Meaning of Life*

Author: Wendy Mass

Book Overview: Left with a gift from his deceased father, but without a key to open the complex box in which is stored, presents a challenge for Jeremy and his best friend, Lizzy.

Book Distinctions: *Publishers Weekly* Starred Review, Junior Library Guild Selection, Voice of Youth Advocates 2007 Top Shelf Fiction for Middle School Readers

AASL Standards for the 21st-Century Learner Standards: 2.1.3 Arrange story events in a graphical organizer

Content Areas: Language Arts, Philosophy

AR Reading Level: 4.5

Author Web Site: http://www.wendymass.com/

Suggested Answers:

1. Jeremy collects mutant candy, while Lizzy is trying to collect a complete deck of cards from missing cards that she finds in public places.

2. Reader response.

3. They were unsuccessful locating keys at the lock shop and the flea market to open the box. So they break into Harold's office. Harold kept the box safe for all of these years, but he misplaced the key. The security guard and policeman find them there, and they receive community service as a punishment.

4. Mabel trades a book signed to her and her best friend by A. A. Milne. She wanted to get a dress so that she didn't end up turning into an old maid. Friendship is her meaning of life. Simon traded some of his mom's Tiffany lamps. He wanted a watch and now finds the meaning of life to be relative. Amos traded his grandfather's telescope so that he could track shoes for MIT. He believes that we are all unique.

5. Lizzy chooses a doll, and Jeremy takes a suitcase with odds and ends inside.

6. They enter the hula hoop contest and earn second place.

7. The fourth key is her gift to Jeremy.

8. There is a handwritten letter from his dad. There is a pile of rocks with an explanation of their significance. There is also a gift for Lizzy.

9. He goes to get a rock. This was the adventure his dad hoped Jeremy would have, and Mr. Oswald was involved with the plan from the start.

10. Reader response.

11. Reader response.

Jeremy Fink and the Meaning of Life
by Wendy Mass

1. Jeremy and Lizzy collect different items. What do they collect?

2. Do you collect anything? If so, what? How did your collection begin? If you don't yet have a collection, what would you choose to collect and why?

3. Why do Lizzy and Jeremy go to Harold's office? Do they complete their goal?

4. While helping Mr. Oswald, Lizzy and Jeremy complete three deliveries. Complete the chart with the item that each person traded, the reason for the trade, and their take on the meaning of life.

Name	Item Traded	Reason for Trade	Their Take on The Meaning Life
Mabel Billingsly			
Simon Rudolph			
Amos Grady			

5. Before Mr. Oswald moves to Florida, what gift do Lizzy and Jeremy select?

6. Lizzy and Jeremy participate in the state fair talent contest. What do they do? Are they successful?

7. What does Lizzy give Jeremy for his thirteenth birthday?

8. Once the box is opened, what contents are inside for Jeremy?

9. Where does Jeremy go by himself? Are you surprised by the ending? Why or why not?

10. What is your take on the meaning of life?

11. Ask three people (friends, family members, or school workers) what they think is the meaning of life.

Title: *A Dog for Life*

Author: L. S. Matthews

Book Overview: After learning that his brother can no longer be near the family dog for health reasons, John embarks on a journey to resolve the situation while helping others.

Book Distinctions: ALA *Booklist* Editors' Choice Books for Youth 2006, *Publishers Weekly* Starred Review, ALA *Booklist* Starred Review, Junior Library Guild Selection

AASL Standards for the 21st-Century Learner Standards: 1.1.4 Locate and assess sources

Content Areas: Language Arts, Science, Mathematics, Health

AR Reading Level: 5.2

Author Web Site: http://www.lsmatthewsonline.co.uk/

Suggested Answers:

1. The doctor says the dog, Mouse, cannot stay in their house.

2. John's mom's idea is to take Mouse to the pound. John wants his uncle to take care of Mouse instead. He thinks that if they ask their uncle on the phone, he will say no. But if John travels to ask in person, he will not refuse to help.

3. 63 pounds, 80 pence. 45 pounds, 35 pence. 37 pounds, 50 pence. Students can find currency converters on the Internet.

4. John frees the ponies at night so that they are no longer used for scientific research.

5. Answers will vary.

6. Individual research will vary.

7. Reader response.

A Dog for Life by L. S. Matthews

1. When John's brother Tom becomes very sick, what order does the doctor give?

2. Why does John leave on a train to get to his uncle's house?

3. How much does a ticket from Highwick to Dunchester cost? How much money does John have? How much does a ticket from Highwick to Brigstow cost? Convert the English pounds to American currency.

4. During the trip, John saves three ponies. How?

5. Who did John meet on his travels? What were they like? What do you think John learned from visiting the different families on his voyage? Create a graphic organizer. Be sure to include Sage's family, Pete's family, and Tom's family.

6. Research obesity or cancer in an encyclopedia or on the Internet. Find information to answer the following questions.

    What are the causes of obesity or cancer?

    What are treatments for it?

    What kind of scientific studies are being conducted about the problem?

    What other facts did you learn?

7. Do you agree with Sage's mom or Pete's dad about scientific ideas and practices? Explain your answer.

Title: *Out of Patience*

Author: Brian Meehl

Book Overview: As the residents of a small town learn more about their past, there is the glimmer of the promise of a brighter future.

Book Distinctions: Junior Library Guild Selection

AASL Standards for the 21st-Century Learner Standards: 4.1.2 Students apply reading to their world

Content Areas: Language Arts, History

AR Reading Level: 4.9

Suggested Answers:

1. Scepter of Satan

2. Toilet plunger

3. Toilet

4. Chart responses and predictions will vary.

Out of Patience by Brian Meehl

1. Twelve year old Jake's dad purchases through eBay the legendary "_____ ____ _____."

2. This was the _____ _____ that led to the town demise long ago.

3. Is the small town of Patience, Kansas, ready for a _____ Museum housing the item responsible for their fall from greatness?

4. What do you know about your town's local history? Look at the historical facts of the town presented in the book and locate information about your own town. Then compare what was taking place at the same time.

Years	Patience, Kansas	Your Hometown:

Now that you have explored the history of your town, imagine its future. What will your town be like …

5 years from now?

10 years from now?

50 years from now?

100 years from now?

From *Active Reading: Activities for Librarians and Teachers* by Beth McGuire. Westport, CT: Libraries Unlimited. Copyright © 2009.

Title: *Miss Spitfire: Reaching Helen Keller*

Author: Sarah Miller

Book Overview: A historical fictional account of the turbulent teaching experiences with Anne Sullivan and Helen Keller supplemented by primary resources highlighting the fruits of diligent efforts.

Book Distinctions: ALA *Booklist* Starred Review, American Library Association Best Books for Young Adults

AASL Standards for the 21st-Century Learner Standards: 1.1.6 Students make inferences about Helen's learning and behavior from information in the novel and then create a report card

Content Areas: History, Language Arts

AR Reading Level: 5.8

Author Web Site: http://www.sarahmillerbooks.com/

Suggested Answers:

1. She has accepted a position to teach six-year-old Helen Keller at her home in Alabama.

2. Reasons may vary, but comments could include the following: Annie and Helen have faced health problems. Annie is half-blind and cross-eyed, while Helen is blind and deaf. Both may feel isolated at times because Annie is an orphan and Helen yearns for attention.

3. Responses may vary but should include that words allow for conversation and interaction with other people.

4. Percy is the servant. He is eager to learn.

5. There are many examples of difficulties. Some include the following: Helen locks Annie in a room, and Annie has to be taken out of the window to exit. Helen hits Annie's mouth and breaks a tooth. Helen throws many tantrums. Helen will eat with her hands or refuse to wash for dinner; Helen's parents do not try to stop this behavior and let their child have her way.

6. Annie also has great success with Helen. When Helen works to teach Percy to spell, this is a huge step forward. Gradually, Annie earns Helen's affection. Annie helps Helen become the first person who is deaf and blind to earn a college degree.

7. Report cards will vary.

Miss Spitfire: Reaching Helen Keller
by Sarah Miller

1. Why is Annie traveling from Massachusetts to Alabama at the start of the novel?

2. Using information from the novel, support the following statement by Annie Sullivan from the book: "We're so alike, Helen and I."

3. In a conversation between Annie and Mrs. Keller, Annie says, "words are a miracle." Explain how words are a miracle.

4. Who is Percy? How does he a role play in teaching Helen?

5. Give at least three examples of the difficulties that Annie has trying to maintain control of the situation and hold Helen's attention.

6. Now provide at least three examples of the successes Annie has in teaching Helen.

7. On another sheet of paper, create a report card for Helen and assess her learning. Be sure to consider and include subject material that she studies, her attitudes, and her behavior.

Title: *Agnes Parker . . . Staying Cool in Middle School*

Author: Kathleen O'Dell

Book Overview: Exploring art expands Agnes's experiences in seventh grade while an exciting and new friendship develops.

Book Distinctions: *Kirkus Reviews* Starred Review, Junior Library Guild Selection

AASL Standards for the 21st-Century Learner Standards: 3.1.3 Students write responses to promote understanding and analysis of a situation

Content Areas: Language Arts, Guidance

AR Reading Level: 3.6

Author Web Site: http://www.kathleenodell.com/

Suggested Answers:

1. Prejean is part of the soccer team, and Agnes serves as the assistant, assistant art-room manager.

2. Reader response based on the book.

3. She will place beautiful and unique things inside. Reader opinion for the contents of their box.

4. "Running for a change." The second part is reader response.

5. Her mother and father are taking time off from each other.

6. She gives the speech. Reader response for the second part.

7. He wouldn't use one before because he had been stuffed into lockers so often. Now he has more confidence.

8. Locker decoration is student opinion.

Agnes Parker … Staying Cool in Middle School
by Kathleen O'Dell

1. As Agnes and her best friend start seventh grade, they each decide to do different after-school activities. In what activity does each character participate?

2. Aram is great at making a far-fetched tale. Help Agnes write a far-fetched tale based on an event from the book.

3. Agnes has an art project to create a Cornell box collection. What will she put in it? What items would you place in a Cornell box?

4. Prejean wants to run for class president and have Agnes be campaign manager. What clever slogan does she come up with? Create one or more additional slogans that would work.

5. Agnes notices that Prejean hasn't been eating. What is bothering her?

6. When Prejean can't make the speech for class president, what does Agnes do? Does that go well?

7. At the end of the story Aram uses a locker. Why is this important?

8. If you had a chance to help decorate Prejean's, Agnes's, and Aram's lockers, how would you do it? You now have a chance to decorate the lockers on the next page.

Title: *The Legend of Bass Reeves: Being the True and Fictional Account of the Most Valiant Marshal in the West*

Author: Gary Paulsen

Book Overview: Playing games may be recreational, but for Bass, games yield freedom and experiences and roles in this historical fiction novel.

Book Distinctions: American Library Association Notable Children's Book 2006, ALA *Booklist* Starred Review, *Publishers Weekly* Starred Review, *Kirkus Reviews* Starred Review, Junior Library Guild Selection

AASL Standards for the 21st-Century Learner Standards: 3.1.6 Provide source citations, 4.1.8 Create a wanted poster to further learn about the world where Bass lived

Content Areas: History, Language Arts

AR Reading Level: 5.8

Suggested Answers:

1. Poker

2. Bass's freedom

3. Bass

4. He leaves alone and travels across the land while being followed.

5. He is asked to serve as a Marshal. He completes roughly three thousand missions.

6. Topics, notes, and poster will vary.

The Legend of Bass Reeves: Being the True and Fictional Account of the Most Valiant Marshal in the West by Gary Paulsen

1. Bass grows up in an unjust world where he lives in slavery. When he is nearly seventeen years old, his master teaches him to play a game. What is the game?

2. One night when his master has been drinking alcohol, they play for high stakes. What are they gambling for?

3. Who wins the game?

4. What becomes of Bass?

5. When Bass is fifty-one years old, what is he asked to do? What is the outcome?

6. Learn more about either Wild Bill Hickok or Wyatt Earp of the Wild West to see the type of people who Bass encountered. Create a wanted poster on the back of this page for one of the people that Bass could be pursuing. Incorporate the sources used in the poster.

   Topic:

   Notes:

Title: *On the Wings of Heroes*

Author: Richard Peck

Book Overview: Civilian life during wartime leads to changes in lifestyles.

Book Distinctions: *Publishers Weekly* Starred Review, *School Library Journal* Starred Review, *Kirkus Reviews* Starred Review

AASL Standards for the 21st-Century Learner Standards: 2.1.1 Analyze several topics from the novel to deduce their role in the historical fiction novel and history

Content Areas: History, Language Arts

AR Reading Level: 4.6

Suggested Answers:

1. Students would gather as many dimes as they could each Thursday to earn War Savings Stamps. Once they put $18.70 cents toward the booklet, they earned a War Bond that would be worth $25.00 in ten years. The selling of War Bonds helped to provide monetary funding for the war.

2. Because more women are working during the day, many students no longer walk home to eat lunch. These children are known as "eight-to-five orphans." This will help allow the work to get done while the men go off to war.

3. Joe DiMaggio leads Bill's calisthenics. DiMaggio missed three baseball seasons while serving in the military.

4. Many items including sugar, rubber, metal, clothes, shoes, meat, cheese, and gas are rationed. If twenty-five pounds of scrap metal was turned in you would receive a ticket to a Saturday matinee from the Varsity club. Ten thousand pounds of paper turned in would earn an Eisenhower medal. Coffee grounds, toothpaste tubes, and cooking fat needed to be recycled. Rationing took place to ensure that the troops had enough supplies, and so families didn't take more than their fair share.

5. All of the merchandise that was made in Japan was destroyed and made into a display. People were told to "Remember Pearl Harbor" while shopping during the Christmas season of 1941. There was a burgeoning hatred toward Japan among numerous American citizens after Pearl Harbor.

6. His mom was eager to receive a telegram to learn about her son. The first telegram reported that he was missing. Later, the second telegram arrived stating that he was alive. Telegrams improved communication.

7. The Hisers work on their victory garden. Families grew their own gardens to support the war.

8. Reader response.

On the Wings of Heroes by Richard Peck

Decide the role of the topics from the novel. Then research more information about the topics using print and database sources.

Topic	Role in Novel	Role in History
1. War Bonds	Students would gather as many dimes as they could each Thursday to earn War Savings Stamps. Once they put $18.70 toward the booklet, they earned a War Bond that would be worth $25.00 in ten years.	The selling of War Bonds helped to pay for the war.
2. Women working in industry during war		
3. Joe DiMaggio in regards to the war effort		
4. Rationing		
5. Made in Japan		
6. Telegram		
7. Victory Garden		

8. Do you feel that similar sacrifices by civilians still occur during war-time situations? Explain.

From *Active Reading: Activities for Librarians and Teachers* by Beth McGuire.
Westport, CT: Libraries Unlimited. Copyright © 2009.

Title: *Johnny and the Bomb*

Author: Terry Pratchett

Book Overview: Given the chance to change history, friends are presented with the challenge to stop the dropping of a bomb.

Book Distinctions: Nestle Children's Book Silver Prize 1996, Junior Library Guild Selection

AASL Standards for the 21st-Century Learner Standards: 3.1.3 Write responses with understanding and further analysis of the situation

Content Areas: History, Language Arts

AR Reading Level: 4.3

Author Web Site: http://www.terrypratchettbooks.com/terry/

Suggested Answers:

1. Mrs. Tachyon is a cart lady. She seems to disappear and reappear almost without explanation. Her cart has old newspapers that look new and pickle jars that might be around fifty years old. In addition, a lot of bags are in the cart.

2. The common trait is that the friends get along. Johnny tends to worry, Kristy is a leader and changes her name when it suits her, Wobbler enjoys computers and is of larger stature, Bigmac looks like trouble and is a skinhead, and Yo-less is interested in reading medical sources.

3. Wobbler meets a boy who thinks he must be a Nazi spy because he is so clueless. The boy throws stones at him.

4. Bigmac takes a car for a drive. With all of the technical devices Bigmac has, the police think that he is a member of the Hitler Youth.

5. Johnny wears his granddad's old clothes from the attic, and Yo-less and Bigmac get their clothes from a theater shop to mirror the styles of the 1940s.

6. An old lady calls Yo-less "Sambo," and a policeman thinks that Kristy is not too bright because she is a girl.

7. The characters are successful. The rest of the essay is reader response.

Johnny and the Bomb by Terry Pratchett

Johnny and his friend travel back to the date a bomb will be dropped on their town, May 21, 1941. Changing one event would alter the entire course of history. Will they work to make a difference? How could they work or leave without being seen to make a difference? Complete the following questions. Use another sheet of paper, if necessary.

1. Who is Mrs. Tacyon? What items does she have in her shopping cart? Create a list.

2. Compare and contrast the friends Johnny, Kristy, Wobbler, Bigmac, and Yo-less.

3. Who does Wobbler meet in the past? Is this a pleasant encounter? Explain?

4. Why is Bigmac taken to the police station? What occurs during the questioning?

5. What changes do the friends make for their next trip to the past?

6. Yo-less and Kristy deal with hurtful stereotypes while in the past. What hardships do they face?

7. Complete the essay question in paragraph form: Were the characters from the book successful in changing history? If you could travel back in time to change an event in history, what event would that be? How would you blend in with the people of that time and accomplish a change? Would it be possible to do?

From *Active Reading: Activities for Librarians and Teachers* by Beth McGuire.
Westport, CT: Libraries Unlimited. Copyright © 2009.

Title: *Beowulf: A Hero's Tale Retold*

Author: James Rumford

Book Overview: An introduction into canonical English literature is presented graphically while preserving the plot and several Old English terms.

Book Distinctions: New York Public Library 100 Titles for Reading and Sharing 2007, *School Library Journal* Best Books Selection 2007, *School Library Journal* Starred Review, *Horn Book* Starred Review, *Horn Book* Fanfare 2007, Junior Library Guild Selection

AASL Standards for the 21st-Century Learner Standards: 4.1.8 Produce artistic interpretations and creative writings to questions

Content Area: Language Arts

AR Reading Level: 4.3

Suggested Answers:

1. Student artwork demonstrates prediction skills.

2. Grendel is an ogre. Their drinking and laughing distracted him.

3. He helped his father before, and they made a pact of friendship.

4. Reader opinion supported by text.

5. Hygelac names him King since he does not have any sons.

6. Someone took the dragon's drinking cup, and it sought revenge.

7. Wiglaf is brave and does not give up.

8. Reader response.

9. Reader response.

Beowulf: A Hero's Tale Retold by James Rumford

1. Before reading, draw what you think an ogre in the book will look like.

[ ]

2. Who is Grendel, and why doesn't he like the Danes?

3. How does Hrothgar know Beowulf?

4. Do you feel that Beowulf fights fairly against Grendel and Grendel's mother? Why or why not?

5. How did Beowulf become the King of the Geats?

6. Many years later Beowulf gets his sword out. What has caused this action?

7. How does Wiglaf help in the fight against the dragon?

8. Using an acrostic, fill in adjectives for each letter of Beowulf's name to describe how he is a hero.

B	
E	
O	
W	
U	
L	
F	

9. Revisit your picture of an ogre. Is your picture of an ogre similar to the work done by James Rumford? How is it different? Draw another picture of an ogre combining both styles.

Title: *Night of the Howling Dogs*

Author: Graham Salisbury

Book Overview: A Boy Scout camping trip turns out to be an arduous test of survival.

Book Distinctions: New York Public Library 100 Titles for Reading and Sharing 2007, ALA *Booklist* Starred Review, Junior Library Guild Selection

AASL Standards for the 21st-Century Learner Standards: 2.1.3 Analyze information and apply current day situations and personal reactions to events

Content Areas: Science, Geography, Language Arts

AR Reading Level: 3.5

Author Web Site: http://www.grahamsalisbury.com/

Suggested Answers:

1. Getting ready for the trip.

2. Vegetation could include naupaka bushes or hau trees. Animals may include sharks or horses.

3. Campfire stories retold will vary.

4. An earthquake and a volcano eruption take place.

5. A shirt is rearranged to serve as shoes.

6. Pahoehoe is dried and smooth while A'a is dried shard and jagged. They encounter both types.

7. Reader response.

1. What are Casey and Dylan getting ready to do at the beginning of the story?

2. Halape is described as a lovely location. Research more about one plant and one animal that are native to the area and complete the chart with your facts.

Vegetation	Animal

3. The group tells stories at the campfire. One story is about the night marchers, and another is about Pele. Choose one of the stories to tell in your own words.

4. What disasters take place during their trip?

5. Give an example of something the scouts used to help themselves survive.

6. Two different types of lava exist. Compare each type. Do the scouts encounter each type of lava? If so, what is the experience?

7. If a badge was awarded to the scout member for the greatest act of heroism, which character would you nominate? Be sure to explain your answer because many of the scouts deserve such an award.

Title: *The Wednesday Wars*

Author: Gary D. Schmidt

Book Overview: Throughout the course of a year, the effects of events in America and Vietnam, school reading, and outings with friends alter Holling's life.

Book Distinctions: Newbery Honor Book, 2008, *Publishers Weekly* Starred Review, *Kirkus Reviews* Starred Review, ALA *Booklist* Starred Review, *Publishers Weekly* Best Children's Books of 2007, *Horn Book* Starred Review

AASL Standards for the 21st-Century Learner Standards: 3.1.3 Students demonstrate an understanding of the novel in both writing and speaking

Content Areas: History, Language Arts

AR Reading Level: 5.9

Suggested Answers:

1. Student readings will vary, but the readings of Holling Hoodhood are taken from the novel.

   Before the school year: *Treasure Island, Kidnapped, Black Arrow, Call of the Wild,* most of *Ivanhoe*

   September: *Treasure Island* (again)

   October: *The Merchant of Venice*

   November: *The Tempest*

   December: *The Tragedy of Macbeth*

   January: *Home Town Chronicle*

   February: *Romeo and Juliet*

   March: *Julius Caesar*

   April: took off

   May: *Hamlet, Prince of Denmark*

   June: *Much Ado about Nothing*

2. 1967; events and people include Vietnam, Martin Luther King, Jr., Bobby Kennedy, Lyndon B. Johnson, Walter Cronkite, Khesanh

3. Mickey Mantle did not sign Holling's baseball because he was wearing his Shakespeare costume and his signing time was up. Along with his friends Danny and Doug, he had the chance to throw a baseball with the Joe Pepitone and Horace Clarke, obtain their autographs, a ticket for opening day, and their caps, and he received Joe's jacket. Pepitone and Clarke become his favorite players. Reader response as to his or her favorite.

4. The Catholic Relief Agency is vandalized with the message "GO HOME VIET CONG." Mai Thi is also teased by the students for eating rats like they believe people in Vietnam did.

5. Hoodhood and Associates won the bid for the new junior high Kowalski-Yankee Stadium contract.

6. Reader response.

7. Reader response.

The Wednesday Wars by Gary D. Schmidt

1. Compare what you have been reading to what Holling reads throughout the school year.

Month	Your Readings	Holling Hoodhood's Readings
Before the school year		
September		
October		
November		
December		
January		
February		
March		
April		
May		
June		

From *Active Reading: Activities for Librarians and Teachers* by Beth McGuire.
Westport, CT: Libraries Unlimited. Copyright © 2009.

2. The novel is set during the year of _____. What are three examples of the events and people that the Hoodhood family learned about by watching the evening news and reading the paper?

   a.

   b.

   c.

3. Who do you think is Holling's favorite baseball player? Explain. Do you have a personal favorite baseball player?

4. Why has the school year been difficult for Mai Thi?

5. What construction bid did Hoodhood and Associates win?

6. Which construction plan would you most like to assist with if given the chance?

7. What are three ideas that you would share with the architecture firm? Create a presentation suitable to share with a firm. Share the presentation with your class.

Title: *The Invention of Hugo Cabret*

Author: Brian Selznick

Book Overview: A combination of art and words sets the stage for the search of automation.

Book Distinctions: Caldecott Medal Winner 2008, National Book Award (Young People's Literature) Finalist 2008, New York Public Library 100 Titles for Reading and Sharing 2007, *Publishers Weekly* Best Children's Books of 2007, Junior Library Guild Selection, *Today Show*'s Al's Book Club for Kids, *Publishers Weekly* Starred Review, *Kirkus Reviews* Starred Review, Best Children's Books 2007, *School Library Journal* Starred Review, Book Sense Children's Picks Spring 2007, *Horn Book* Starred Review, Quill Children's Chapter/Middle Grade Award Winner

AASL Standards for the 21st-Century Learner Standards: 3.1.6 Provide source citations, 4.1.8 Respond to questions by drawing answers

Content Areas: Language Arts, History

AR Reading Level: 5.1

Author Web Site: http://www.theinventionofhugocabret.com/about_brian_bio.htm

Suggested Answers:

Picture renditions will vary.

1. His dad dies in a fire while trying to fix automation in a museum attic.

2. Hugo changes clocks.

3. He purchases a magic book.

4. They find pictures by Georges Méliès.

5. He visits to watch an old movie that they believe the toymaker produced.

6. Favorite part is a reader opinion.

7. Student selections and responses will differ based on topic.

The Invention of Hugo Cabret
by Brian Selznick

Answer the following questions by drawing your response. Use captions to add explanation and detail.

1. What happens to Hugo's dad?

2. Hugo stays with his uncle. What does Hugo do to pass time?

3. Etienne gives Hugo money to buy something special. What does Hugo purchase?

4. Isabelle and Hugo find something unique in the armoire. What do they find?

5. Why does the professor visit the toymaker at his house?

6. What is your favorite part of the book?

7. Select one of the following topics to research and create a scene: Tom Mix, Louise Brooks, Charlie Chaplin, Jean Renoir, Buster Keaton. What source did you use?

Title: *The Mailbox*

Author: Audrey Shafer

Book Overview: Gabe's Uncle Vernon takes care of him until Vernon dies. A stranger then helps Gabe survive, while also shedding light on the courageous life of Uncle Vernon.

Book Distinctions: Junior Library Guild Selection

AASL Standards for the 21st-Century Learner Standards: 1.1.4 Locate, assess and summarize information

Content Areas: History, Language Arts

AR Reading Level: 5.0

Author Web Site: http://www.ashafer.com/home.html

Suggested Answers:

1. He is reclusive and veteran of the Vietnam War.

2. He finds his uncle dead.

3. A letter is in the mailbox and his uncle's body is gone.

4. He was a decorated soldier and awarded the Purple Heart.

5. It is awarded to a serviceman who is injured or killed in combat.

6. George Washington (Badge of Military Merit), 1782

7. Douglas MacArthur

8. About 1.7 million

9. Picture of the Purple Heart

The Mailbox by Audrey Shafer

1. Twelve-year-old Gabe lives with his Uncle Vernon. Describe Uncle Vernon.

   _____

   _____

   _____

2. What happens on the morning of Gabe's second day of sixth grade?

   _____

   _____

   _____

   _____

3. What does Gabe find in the mailbox and the house when he returns from school?

   _____

   _____

   _____

   _____

4. As Gabe misses Vernon, he learns more about Vernon's life. What does he learn?

   _____

   _____

   _____

   _____

   Use a variety of sources including the encyclopedia, databases, and the Purple Heart organization (www.purpleheart.org) to find the answers to the following questions.

5. How can someone earn the Purple Heart?

   _____

   _____

   _____

   _____

6. Who first started bestowing the award that would later be called the Purple Heart? In what year?

_____

_____

_____

_____

7. What general worked diligently to see that the Purple Heart would be instituted?

_____

_____

_____

_____

8. About how many Purple Hearts have been issued up to this date?

_____

_____

_____

_____

9. Draw a picture of the Purple Heart Medal.

Title: *Encyclopedia Brown Cracks the Case*

Author: Donald J. Sobol

Illustrator: James Bernardin

Book Overview: The classic character delivers more cases to future sleuths.

Book Distinctions: Junior Library Guild Selection

AASL Standards for the 21st-Century Learner Standards: 2.1.3 Arrange story events in a graphical organizer

Content Area: Language Arts

AR Reading Level: 4.8

Suggested Answers:

1. Leroy is in fifth grade and ten years old. His father is a police chief and often asks Leroy for his advice on work-related situations. Leroy Brown is his real name, but children always call him by his nickname, Encyclopedia Brown.

2. Prediction

3. Their answers may vary according to their clues. The way that Encyclopedia solves the case can include the following:

    A. Onion juice seals the deal.
    B. The author's last name is Lewis, not Louis.
    C. Bully can't frame them with his big mouth.
    D. George Washington did not sign the Constitution.
    E. Butterflies were not swarming the tree.
    F. The relative rigged the contest.
    G. Duck can't survive in space.
    H. The owner wanted to collect the sizeable insurance money.
    I. There would be no more mission donation money for houses.
    J. The stamps to attract more people to her museum.

4. Individual response.

Encyclopedia Brown Cracks the Case
by Donald J. Sobol, illustrated by James Bernardin

1. Describe Leroy.

2. Encyclopedia solves ten mysteries in this novel. Predict how many mysteries you will be able to solve on your own from the novel. _____ /10

3. Keep track of your clues as you read the chapters. Then go to the back of the book for the solution and see if your hunch is correct.

Case	Clues for you to solve the mystery	How Encyclopedia Brown solves the case
A. Forgetful Jewel Thief		
B. Autographed *Alice in Wonderland*		
C. Lemonade Stand		
D. Revolutionary Treasures		
E. Missing Butterfly Brooch		
F. Counterfeit Dough		
G. Astronaut Duck		
H. Lucky Catch		
I. Missing Money		
J. Stolen Confederate Stamps		

4. How many mysteries did you solve on your own? _____ /10.

Title: *Eggs*

Author: Jerry Spinelli

Book Overview: Two unlikely individuals form life-changing friendships and tackle some of their deepest fears.

Book Distinctions: *Kirkus Reviews* Starred Review, Junior Library Guild Selection

AASL Standards for the 21st-Century Learner Standards: 3.1.5 Students apply their local geographic area to learning

Content Area: Language Arts

AR Reading Level: 3.6

Author Web Site: http://www.jerryspinelli.com/newbery_002.htm

Suggested Answers:

1. She died because of a wet floor. He lives with his grandma.

2. Primrose lives in a van.

3. Foot readings should generate a creative response.

4. They go hunting for worms.

5. She dresses like an adult. They do not get scared. Personal responses to public libraries will be different. At the present time, the Kids' Zone tools section of the National Center for Educational Statistics is a helpful place to locate libraries: http://nces.ed.gov/nceskids/tools/library/index.asp

6. She wants to repaint her room.

7. Reader response.

8. Reader response, but should mention friendship as one of the benefits.

Eggs by Jerry Spinelli

1. What happened to David's mother? As a result, who does he live with?

2. Where does Primrose live?

3. Pretend that you are Primrose and read your foot. Tell your fortune below.

4. What do David and Primrose do that helps ease David's fear of the dark?

5. How do David and Primrose get into the public library scare event? Did they get scared?

    What is your nearest public library?

    Locate their web address as well.

    What is one upcoming event that interests you?

6. Why do they work so hard to get the funds to buy paint?

7. Is there something that you would like to have so much that you would sell items at a rummage sell?

8. How do both David and Primrose benefit from knowing each other?

Title: *The Mysterious Benedict Society*

Author: Trenton Stewart

Illustrator: Carson Ellis

Book Overview: A gifted group of children work as a team to take on a controlling innovator.

Book Distinctions: *School Library Journal* Best Books Selection 2007, ALA *Booklist* Starred Review, *Publishers Weekly* Starred Review, *School Library Journal* Starred Review, *Bulletin of the Center for Children's Books* Starred Review, Voice of Youth Advocates 2007 Top Shelf Fiction for Middle School Readers

AASL Standards for the 21st-Century Learner Standards: 2.1.5 Work with a partner to provide feedback on a test that student creates

Content Areas: Language Arts, Guidance

AR Reading Level: 5.6

Book-Related Web site: http://www.mysteriousbenedictsociety.com/content/index.asp

Suggested Answers:

1. Tests: a) paper and pencil; b) forty-question timed test, share pencil, tempted to cheat; c) not to step on blue or black floor squares; d) reach staircase, climb steps, ring bell; e) see how the children react when hungry and tired.

    Reader opinion for the grades; responses may include the following: Reynie has problem-solving skills. Kate has ingenuity. Sticky has a wonderful memory. Constance is exceedingly truthful.

2. Reader response to items that they carry. Kate always carries her bucket. Items inside include a Swiss Army knife, a flashlight, a penlight, extra-strength glue, marbles, a slingshot, fishing twine, a pencil, an eraser, a kaleidoscope, and a horseshoe magnet.

3. Morse code in secret.

4. He is their bodyguard and lost his memories when escaping years ago.

5. Reader opinion.

6. Powerful ways to control the brain.

7. Teamwork.

8. Reader response and partner work. Students can also make their quiz interactive using Web tools.

The Mysterious Benedict Society
by Trenton Stewart, illustrated by Carson Ellis

1. What types of test do the children take? Of the children who passed the tests, whom do you think should receive the highest grade? Explain.

2. Are there certain items that you always take with you? What does Kate carry at all times?

3. How will they communicate with Benedict undercover in the Learning Institute for the Very Enlightened?

4. Who is Milligan, and what happened to him?

5. Constance picks their group name: "The Mysterious Benedict Society." Do you think this is a well-chosen name? If not, what name would you have chosen?

6. What is Mr. Curtain trying to accomplish?

7. How does The Mysterious Benedict Society stop Mr. Curtain's plan?

8. Create a new test for entrance into The Mysterious Benedict Society for potential candidates. Share with a classmate who can take the quiz and offer suggestions.

From *Active Reading: Activities for Librarians and Teachers* by Beth McGuire.
Westport, CT: Libraries Unlimited. Copyright © 2009.

Title: *Emma-Jean Lazarus Fell Out of a Tree*

Author: Lauren Tarshis

Book Overview: Emma-Jean tries to do the right things by using a logical approach, but her peers often misunderstand this method.

Book Distinctions: *School Library Journal* Best Books Selection 2007, *Publishers Weekly* Best Children's Books of 2007, Junior Library Guild Selection, *Publishers Weekly* Starred Review, *School Library Journal* Starred Review, Book Sense Children's Picks Spring 2007, 2008 Golden Kite Honor Book for Fiction

AASL Standards for the 21st-Century Learner Standards: 1.1.3 Create a question-and-answer section for the school newspaper

Content Areas: Language Arts, Guidance, Philosophy

AR Reading Level: 5.2

Author Web site: http://www.laurentarshis.com/

Suggested Answers:

1. He died in an accident on I-95. He was to give a presentation at a math conference about Jules Henri.

2. Emma-Jean makes Laura believe that she's been invited to a basketball function the same time as the ski trip. Emma-Jean makes the invitation look as authentic as possible, but there is no such event. Reader response for the next part.

3. She is named after the woman who wrote the poem for the Statue of Liberty. Her parents decided to get married when visiting the statue. Reader response for their own name.

4. She finds that a mouse is eating the candy.

5. She tries to make the situation right again.

6. Student-created newspaper section in Emma-Jean's persona.

Emma-Jean Lazarus Fell Out of a Tree
by Lauren Tarshis

1. Emma-Jean loved her dad very much, but tragedy occurred two years ago. What happened to her dad? Where was he going?

2. How does Emma-Jean help Colleen get back her best friend? Do you think this was a good strategy? Why or why not?

3. How did her parents select Emma-Jean's name? Do you know why you were given your name? Try to find out and write below.

4. How does Emma-Jean prove that Will Keeler is innocent?

5. Why is Emma-Jean in a tree at Colleen's house in the first place? What happens?

6. Think of an issue that people are talking about in school. How would Emma-Jean try to solve the problem? Create a question-and-answer section in the tone of Emma-Jean that is suitable to publish in the school newspaper.

From *Active Reading: Activities for Librarians and Teachers* by Beth McGuire.
Westport, CT: Libraries Unlimited. Copyright © 2009.

Title: *Pete and Fremont*

Author: Jenny Tripp

Illustrator: John Manders

Book Overview: If life seems like a circus, imagine how it must feel to be a star performer in a circus act about to be taken out of the spotlight.

AASL Standards for the 21st-Century Learner Standards: 4.1.8 Create an agenda for the act

Content Area: Language Arts

AR Reading Level: 4.1

Illustrator Web Site: http://www.johnmanders.com/

Suggested Answers:

1. He is getting older and struggling to jump through a fire hoop without catching fire.

2. He can juggle. Reader response as to particular skills.

3. They train the bear secretly and save food for Fremont.

4. They star in the show together.

5. Reader response.

Pete and Fremont
by Jenny Tripp, illustrated by John Manders

1. Why is Pete, Pierre le Chien, losing his spot as the big finale?

2. Fremont, the bear, is not happy being caged up. Pete learns that Fremont has a talent. What talent does he have? If you needed to take part in a circus, what act would you do?

3. How do all of the animals try to save Fremont? Are they successful?

4. Rita, the chimp, and Pete begin to get along better. What do they do?

5. Create an agenda for the upcoming act staring Rita and Pete with a special appearance from Fremont. This agenda will be posted around town to excite the public about the act.

From *Active Reading: Activities for Librarians and Teachers* by Beth McGuire.
Westport, CT: Libraries Unlimited. Copyright © 2009.

Title: *A Crooked Kind of Perfect*

Author: Linda Urban

Book Overview: Learning to play the piano well becomes Zoe's goal.

Book Distinctions: Book Sense Children's Picks Fall 2007, New York Public Library 100 Titles for Reading and Sharing 2007, Junior Library Guild Selection

AASL Standards for the 21st-Century Learner Standards: 1.1.8 Skillfully use and locate print and nonprint resources to further their research project; 3.1.6 Provide source citations

Content Areas: Music, Language Arts

AR Reading Level: 3.9

Author Web Site: http://www.lindaurbanbooks.com/

Suggested Answers:

1. Her dad takes many classes including:
   - Make Friends and Profit while Scrapbooking
   - Earn Bucks Driving Trucks
   - Party Smarty: Turn Social Events into Cash Money
   - Scuba-Dooba-Do
   - Golden Gloves: Make a Mint Coaching Boxing
   - Roger, Wilco, Over, and Cash! Learn to Fly Like Pros

   Individual class selection is reader response.

2. This is one of the biggest honors to a performer. She thinks it will be perfect. Student research follows.

3. She believes that he is the best piano player and has great records. Research follows.

4. No, she isn't excited and seems to be looking for something else when opening the gift. Joella Tinstella is now her best friend.

6. Reader response.

7. It is a competition. Yes.

8. The title is mentioned on page 117. Reader selection for a different title.

A Crooked Kind of Perfect by Linda Urban

1. What are some of the Living Room Courses that Zoe's dad takes?

    a.

    b.

    c.

    Which class would you like to take the most?

2. Why does Zoe dream of being in Carnegie Hall? What does she imagine it would be like to be there?

    Research: Who has performed at Carnegie Hall in the past, and who will be there in the near future? Locate facts and images, and cite the source.

3. Zoe looks up to Vladimir Horowitz. According to what you read in the novel, why does she feel this way?

    Can you think of other reasons? Conduct research about Horowitz. Cite your sources.

4. Do you think that Emma likes her birthday gift of toe-socks? Why?

5. Is Emma, Wheeler, or Colton a more loyal friend to Zoe? What examples from the book lead you to believe this?

6. No hit music from the 1980s is an option for Zoe to play. Can you locate any hit music from the 1980s that would play well on a piano? Be sure to write down the year the song was released and the artist or group responsible for it.

7. Zoe makes it to the Perform-O-Rama. What is that? Does she have fun?

8. When is the title of the book mentioned in the novel? If you could rename the book, what title would you recommend?

From *Active Reading: Activities for Librarians and Teachers* by Beth McGuire.
Westport, CT: Libraries Unlimited. Copyright © 2009.

Title: *Chaucer's Canterbury Tales*

Author: Retold and illustrated by Marcia Williams

Book Overview: A selection of classic English literature with a new and appealing look.

Book Distinctions: *School Library Journal* Best Books 2007 selection

AASL Standards for the 21st-Century Learner Standards: 3.1.3 Write a story in similar fashion of the novel and share with the class

Content Area: Language Arts

AR Reading Level: 6.3

Suggested Answers:

1. e
2. a
3. h
4. f
5. c
6. i
7. d
8. b
9. g
10. They are leaving London to visit the tomb of Saint Thomas Becket in Canterbury.
11. Reader response for best tale. The travelers could not select their favorite tale.
12. Reader response. Students will also draw a picture.

Chaucer's Canterbury Tales
Retold and illustrated by Marcia Williams

Match the story descriptions to the appropriate tales.

Story	Story Clue
_____ 1. The Knight's Tale	a. A humorous trick revolving around a flood ploy.
_____ 2. The Miller's Tale	b. Death is found.
_____ 3. The Reeve's Tale	c. A dishonest friar is given a stinky donation.
_____ 4. The Wife of Bath's Tale	d. Magic with rocks.
_____ 5. The Summoner's Tale	e. Royal cousins fight over a maiden.
_____ 6. The Clerk's Tale	f. A knight's life is saved by solving a riddle.
_____ 7. The Franklin's Tale	g. A good voice and a dream go far.
_____ 8. The Pardoner's Tale	h. Flour revenge.
_____ 9. The Nun's Priest's Tale	i. Long live loyalty.

10. To what destination and for what reason are these storytellers traveling?

11. Which tale do you think is the best? Why? Was this the travelers' favorite tale?

12. If you were to take a trip and write about it, what would the title of your work be? What tale would you share? Write your story on the back of this sheet and include an illustration. Read your tale to the class.

Bibliography

Nonfiction

Aronson, Marc. *Up Close: Robert F. Kennedy, a Twentieth-Century Life.* New York: Viking, 2007. 204p. $15.99. ISBN 978-0-670-06066-5.

Bardoe, Cheryl. Illustrated by Jos. A. Smith. *Gregor Mendel: The Friar Who Grew Peas.* New York: Abrams Books for Young Readers, 2006. Np. $18.95. ISBN 978-0-8109-5475-5.

Burns, Loree Griffin. *Tracking Trash: Flotsam, Jetsam, and the Science of Ocean Motion.* Boston: Houghton Mifflin, 2007. 56p. $18.00. ISBN 978-0-618-58131-3.

Collard, Sneed B., III. *Pocket Babies and Other Amazing Marsupials.* Plain City, OH: Darby Creek, 2007. 72p. $18.95. ISBN 978-1-58196-046-4.

Cook, Sally, and James Charlton. Illustrated by Ross MacDonald. *Hey Batta Batta Swing! The Wild Old Days of Baseball.* New York: M.K. McElderry Books, 2007, 48p. $17.99. ISBN 978-1-41691207-1.

Curlee, Lynn. *Skyscraper.* New York: Atheneum, 2007. $17.99. 42p. ISBN 978-0-689-84489-8.

Freedman, Russell. *Freedom Walkers: The Story of the Montgomery Bus Boycott.* New York: Holiday House, 2006. $18.95. 114p. ISBN 0-8234-2031-0.

Gore, Al. *An Inconvenient Truth: The Crisis of Global Warming Adapted for a New Generation.* New York: Viking, 2006. 191p. $16.00p. ISBN 978-0-670-06272-0.

Grogan, John. *Marley: A Dog Like No Other* (adapted for young readers). New York: HarperCollins, 2007. 196p. $16.99. ISBN 0-06-124033-8.

Hampton, Wilborn. *War in the Middle East, A Reporter's Story: Black September and the Yom Kippur War.* Cambridge, MA: Candlewick, 2007. 112p. $19.99. ISBN 978-0-763624934.

Lasky, Kathryn. Illustrated by Stan Fellows. *John Muir: America's First Environmentalist.* Cambridge, MA: Candlewick, 2006. 41p. $16.99. ISBN 0-7636-1957-4.

McClafferty, Carla Killough. *Something Out of Nothing: Marie Curie and Radium.* New York: Farrar, Straus & Giroux, 2006. 134p. $18.00. ISBN 978-0-374-38036-6.

Montgomery, Sy. Photographs by Nic Bishop. *Quest for the Tree Kangaroo: An Expedition to the Cloud Forest of New Guinea.* Boston: Houghton Mifflin, 2006. 79p. $18.00. ISBN 978-0618-49641-9.

Nau, Thomas. *Walker Evans: Photographer of America.* New Milford, CT: Roaring Brook Press, 2007. 63 p. $19.95. ISBN 978-1-59643-225-3.

O'Brien, Patrick. *The Mutiny on the Bounty.* New York: Walker and Company, 2007. Np. $17.95. ISBN 0-8027-9587-0.

Rockwell, Anne. Illustrated by Lizzy Rockwell. *Who Lives in an Alligator Hole?* New York: HarperCollins, 2006. 33p. $15.99. ISBN 0-06-028530-3.

Singer, Marilyn. *Venom.* Plain City, OH: Darby Creek, 2007. 96p. $19.95. ISBN 978-1-58196-043-3.

Sullivan, Edward T. *The Ultimate Weapon: A Race to Develop the Atomic Bomb.* New York: Holiday House, 2007. 182p. $24.95. ISBN 978-0-8234-1855-8.

Thimmesh, Catherine. *Team Moon: How 400,000 People Landed Apollo 11 on the Moon.* Boston: Houghton Mifflin, 2006. 80p. $19.95. ISBN 978-0618-50757-3.

Treaster, Joseph, B. *Hurricane Force: In the Path of America's Deadliest Storms.* (A New York Times Book). Boston: Kingfisher, 2007. 128p. $16.95. ISBN 978-0-75346086-3.

Fiction

Alexander, Lloyd. *The Golden Dream of Carlo Chuchio.* New York: Henry Holt, 2007. 306p. $18.95. ISBN 978-0-8050-8333-0.

Auch, MJ. *One-Handed Catch.* New York: Henry Holt, 2006. 248p. $16.95. ISBN 978-0-8050-7900-5.

Avi. Illustrated by Karina Raude. *The Traitor's Gate: A Novel.* New York: Atheneum, 2007. 353p. $17.99. ISBN 978-0-689-85335-7.

Boyce, Frank Cottrell. *Framed.* New York: HarperCollins, 2006. 306p. $17.89. ISBN 0-06-073403-5 (first published 2005).

Carman, Patrick. *Atherton: The House of Power.* New York: Little, Brown and Company, 2007. 330p. $16.99. ISBN 978-0-316-16670-6.

Clippinger, Carol. *Open Court.* New York: Alfred A. Knopf, 2007. 259p. (262 with acknowledgements). $15.99. ISBN 978-0-375-84049-4.

Creech, Sharon. Illustrated by David Diaz. *The Castle Corona.* New York: Joanna Cotler Books, 2007, 320p. $18.99. ISBN 978-0-06-084621-3.

DiCamillo, Kate. Illustrated by Bagram Ibatoulline. *The Miraculous Journey of Edward Tulane.* Cambridge, MA: Candlewick, 2006. 198p. $18.99. ISBN 0-7636-2589-2.

Feinstein, John. *Vanishing Act: Mystery at the U.S. Open.* New York: Alfred A. Knopf, 2006. 279p. $16.95. ISBN 978-0-375-83592-6.

Fleischman, Sid. *The Entertainer and the Dybbuk.* New York: Greenwillow Books, 2007. 175p. $17.89. ISBN 978-0-06-134446-6.

Green, Tim. *Football Genius.* New York: HarperCollins, 2007. 244p. $16.99. ISBN 978-0-06-112270-5.

Hartnett, Sonya. Illustrated by Don Powers. *The Silver Donkey.* Cambridge, MA: Candlewick Press, 2006. 266p. $15.99. ISBN 978-0-7636-2937-3.

Hawking, Lucy, and Stephen Hawking. Also with Christophe Galfard, Ph.D. Illustrated by Garry Parsons. *George's Secret Key to the Universe.* New York: Simon & Schuster Books for Young Readers, 2007. 297p. $17.99. ISBN 978-1-4169-5462-0.

Heldring, Thatcher. *Toby Wheeler: Eighth-Grade Benchwarmer.* New York: Delacorte Press, 2007. 211p. $14.99. ISBN 978-0-385-73390-8.

Holm, Jennifer L. Pictures by Elicia Castaldi. *Middle School Is Worse than Meatloaf: A Year Told through Stuff.* New York: Atheneum Books for Young Readers, 2007. Np. $12.99. ISBN 978-0-689-85281-7.

Kadohata, Cynthia. *Cracker!: The Best Dog in Vietnam.* New York: Atheneum, 2007. 308p. $16.99. ISBN 978-1-4169-0637-7.

Keehn, Sally M. *Magpie Gabbard and the Quest for the Buried Moon.* New York: Philomel Books, 2007. 198p. $16.99. ISBN 978-0-399-24340-0.

Kennedy, Marlane. *Me and the Pumpkin Queen.* New York: Greenwillow Books, 2007. 187p. $16.89. ISBN 978-0-06-114023-5.

Kinney, Jeff. *Diary of a Wimpy Kid.* New York: Amulet Books, 2007. 217p. $12.95. ISBN 978-0-8109-9313-6.

Kladstrup, Kristin. *The Book of Story Beginnings.* Cambridge, MA: Candlewick Press, 2006. 360p. $15.99. ISBN 0-7636-2609-0.

Korman, Gordon. *Schooled.* New York: Hyperion Books for Children, 2007. 208p. $15.99. ISBN 978-0786856923.

Konigsburg, E. L. *The Mysterious Edge of the Heroic World.* New York: Antheneum Books for Young Readers, 2007. 244p. $16.99. ISBN 978-1-4169-4972-5.

LaFevers, R. L. Illustrated by Yoko Tanaka. *Theodosia and the Serpents of Chaos.* Boston: Houghton Mifflin, 2007. 344p. $16.99. ISBN 978-0-618-75638-4.

Laybourn, Emma. *Missing Magic.* New York: Dial Books, 2007. 182p. $16.99. ISBN 978-0-8037-3219-3.

Levine, Gail Carson. *Fairest.* New York: HarperCollins, 2006. 326p. $16.99. ISBN 0-06-073408-6.

Lowry, Lois. *Gossamer.* Boston: Houghton Mifflin, 2006. 140p. $16.99. ISBN 978-0-618-68550-9.

Maguire, Gregory. *What-the-Dickens: The Story of a Rogue Tooth Fairy.* Cambridge, MA: Candlewick, 2007. 295p. $15.99. ISBN 978-0-7636-2961-8.

Mass, Wendy. *Jeremy Fink and the Meaning of Life.* New York: Little, Brown and Company, 2006. 289p. $15.99. ISBN 978-0-316-05829-2.

Matthews, L. S. *A Dog for Life.* New York: Delacorte Press, 2006. 167p. $15.00. ISBN 0-385-73366-6.

Meehl, Brian. *Out of Patience.* New York: Delacorte Press, 2006. 292p. $15.95. ISBN 0-385-73299-6.

Miller, Sarah. *Miss Spitfire: Reaching Helen Keller.* New York: Atheneum Books, 2007. 208p. $16.99. ISBN 978-1-4169-2542-2.

O'Dell, Kathleen. *Agnes Parker ... Staying Cool in Middle School.* New York: Dial, 2007. 156p. $16.99. ISBN 978-0-8037-3078-6.

Paulsen, Gary. *Legend of Bass Reeves: Being the True and Fictional Account of the Most Valiant Marshal in the West.* New York: Wendy Lamb Books, 2006. 137p. $15.95. ISBN 978-0-385-74661-8.

Peck, Richard. *On the Wings of Heroes.* New York: Dial Books, 2007. 148p. $16.99. ISBN 978-0-8037-3081-6.

Pratchett, Terry. *Johnny and the Bomb.* New York: HarperCollins, 2007. 245p. $17.89. ISBN 978-0-06-054192-7.

Rumford, James. *Beowulf: A Hero's Tale Retold.* Boston: Houghton Mifflin, 2007. Np. $17.00. ISBN 978-0-618-75637-7.

Salisbury, Graham. *Night of the Howling Dogs.* New York: Wendy Lamb Books, 2007. 185p. $16.99. ISBN 978-0-385-73122-5.

Schmidt, Gary D. *The Wednesday Wars.* New York: Clarion Books, 2007. 264p. $16.00. ISBN 978-0-618-72483-3.

Selznick, Brian. *The Invention of Hugo Cabret.* New York: Scholastic, 2007. 533p. $22.95. ISBN 978-0-439-81378-5.

Shafer, Audrey. *The Mailbox.* New York: Delacorte Press, 2006. 178p. $15.95. ISBN 978-0-385-733441.

Sobol, Donald J. Illustrated by James Bernardin. *Encyclopedia Brown Cracks the Case.* New York: Dutton Children's Books, 2007. 90p. $15.99. ISBN 978-0-525-47924-6.

Spinelli, Jerry. *Eggs.* New York: Little, Brown and Company, 2007. 220p. $15.99. ISBN 978-0-316-16646-1.

Stewart, Trenton Lee. Illustrated by Carson Ellis. *The Mysterious Benedict Society.* New York: Little, Brown and Company, 2007. 485p. $16.99. ISBN 978-0-316-05777-6.

Tarshis, Lauren. *Emma-Jean Lazarus Fell Out of a Tree.* New York: Dial Books, 2007. 199p. $16.99. ISBN 978-0-8037-3164-6.

Tripp, Jenny. Illustrated by John Manders. *Pete and Fremont.* Orlando, FL: Harcourt, 2007. 180p. $16.00. ISBN 978-0-15-205629-2.

Urban, Linda. *A Crooked Kind of Perfect.* New York: Harcourt, 2007. 211p. $16.00. ISBN 978-0-15-206007-7.

Williams, Marcia, retold. *Chaucer's Canterbury Tales.* Cambridge, MA: Candlewick Press, 2007. 45p. $16.99. ISBN 978-0-7636-3197-0.

Webliography

Author/Illustrator Web Sites

Note: All Web sites were active at the time of publication.

Nonfiction Books

Aronson, Marc. http://www.marcaronson.com/.

Bardoe, Cheryl. http://www.cherylbardoe.com/.

Bishop, Nic. "Nic Bishop: Author and Photographer of Nature Books for Children." http://www.nicbishop.com/.

Burns, Loree Griffin. "Loree Burns: Children's Author." http://www.loreeburns.com/.

Collard, Sneed B., III. http://www.author-illustr-source.com/sneedbcollard.htm

Cook, Sally. http://members.authorsguild.net/sallycook/.

Curlee, Lynn. http://curleeart.com/.

Gore, Al. http://www.algore.com/.

Grogan, John. "Marley and Me." HarperCollins Web site. http://www.marleyandme.com/.

Lasky, Kathryn. http://www.kathrynlasky.com/.

Mansfield, Howard, and Sy Montgomery. "Authorwire: The Website of Howard Mansfied and Sy Montgomery." http://www.authorwire.com/.

McClafferty, Carla. http://www.carlamcclafferty.com/.

O'Brien, Patrick. http://www.patrickobrienstudio.com/index.html.

Rockwell, Anne. http://www.annerockwell.com.

Singer, Marilyn. http://www.marilynsinger.net/biblio.htm.

Smith, Jos. A. "The Art of Jos. A. Smith." http://josasmith.com/Artist.asp?ArtistID=5617&Akey=QSH5QVDH.

Sullivan, Edward T. http://www.sully-writer.com/.

Thimmesh, Catherine. http://www.catherinethimmesh.com/.

Fiction Books

Avi. http://www.avi-writer.com/.

Carman, Patrick. http://www.patrickcarman.com/main/index.html.

Creech, Sharon. http://www.sharoncreech.com/index.html.

DiCamillo, Kate. http://www.katedicamillo.com/.

Fleischman, Sid. http://www.sidfleischman.com/.

Green, Tim. http://www.timgreenbooks.com/.

Heldring, Thatcher. http://thatchertheauthor.com/.

Holm, Jennifer. http://www.jenniferholm.com/.

Kadohata, Cynthia. http://www.kira-kira.us/.

Keehn, Sally. http://www.sallykeehn.com/.

Kennedy, Marlane. http://www.marlanekennedy.com/.

Kinney, Jeff. http://www.wimpykid.com/.

Korman, Gordon. http://gordonkorman.com.

LaFevers, R. L. http://www.rllafevers.com/about.html.

Lowry, Lois. http://www.loislowry.com/.

Manders, John. http://www.johnmanders.com/.

Mass, Wendy. http://www.wendymass.com/.

Matthews, L. S. http://www.lsmatthewsonline.co.uk/.

Miller, Sarah. http://www.sarahmillerbooks.com/.

O'Dell, Kathleen. http://www.kathleenodell.com/.

Pratchett, Terry. "TerryPratchettBooks.com." HarperCollins. http://www.terrypratchettbooks.com/terry/.

Raude, Karina. http://karinaraude.com/index.html.

Salisbury, Graham. http://www.grahamsalisbury.com/.

Selznick, Brian. http://www.theinventionofhugocabret.com/about_brian_bio.htm.

Shafer, Audrey. http://www.ashafer.com/home.html.

Spinelli, Jerry. http://www.jerryspinelli.com/newbery_002.htm.

Tarshis, Lauren. http://www.laurentarshis.com/.

Urban, Linda. http://www.lindaurbanbooks.com/.

Book-Related Web Sites

Simon and Schuster, Inc. http://www.secretkeytotheuniverse.com/.

"The Curiosity Chronicles." Hachette Book Group USA. www.AuthorsOnTheWeb.com.

"The Mysterious Benedict Society." http://www.mysteriousbenedictsociety.com/content/index.asp.

Web Sites Related to Activities

Bigpumpkin.com. http://www.bigpumpkin.com/.

"CNN.com." Cable News Network. http://www.cnn.com/.

"Comic Strips for Fun." http://www.comeeko.com.

"Create a Graph." National Center for Educational Statistics. http://nces.ed.gov/nceskids/createagraph/.

"Daily Highs and Lows: National Temperature Extremes." *USA Today.* http://www.usatoday.com/weather/wext.htm.

"Find a Library." National Center for Educational Statistics. http://nces.ed.gov/nceskids/tools/library/index.asp.

"Flicker." Yahoo! Inc. http://www.flickr.com.

"Gloster-Poster Yourself." http://www.glogster.com/.

Google Lit Trips: http://googlelittrips.com

Military Order of the Purple Heart. http://www.purpleheart.org/Membership/default.aspx.

National Baseball Hall of Fame. http://web.baseballhalloffame.org/index.jsp.

Smilebox: http://www.smilebox.com

United States Tennis Association. http://www.usopen.org/home/default.sps.

Resources

Accelerated Reader BookFind: http://www.arbookfind.com

"AASL Standards for the 21st-Century Learner." American Association of School Librarians. http://www.ala.org/ala/aasl/aaslproftools/learningstandards/standards.cfm.

Accelerated Reader (AR) Reading Levels—Nonfiction

AR Level	Book Title
4.4	*Who Lives in an Alligator Hole?*
4.9	*Marley: A Dog Like No Other*, adapted for young readers
5.3	*Quest for the Tree Kangaroo: An Expedition to the Cloud Forest of New Guinea*
5.6	*The Mutiny on the Bounty*
5.8	*Hey Batta Batta Swing!: The Wild Old Days of Baseball*
6	*Gregor Mendel: The Friar Who Grew Peas*
6.1	*John Muir: America's First Environmentalist*
7	*Pocket Babies and Other Amazing Marsupials*
7.1	*Walker Evans: Photographer of America*
7.4	*An Inconvenient Truth: The Crisis of Global Warming*, adapted for a New Generation
7.4	*War in the Middle East, a Reporter's Story: Black September and the Yom Kippur War*
7.5	*Team Moon: How 400,000 People Landed Apollo 11 on the Moon*
7.7	*Freedom Walkers: The Story of the Montgomery Bus Boycott*
7.8	*Venom*
8	*Up Close: Robert F. Kennedy, a Twentieth-Century Life*
8.3	*Something Out of Nothing: Marie Curie and Radium*
8.3	*Hurricane Force: In the Path of America's Deadliest Storms*
8.5	*Tracking Trash: Flotsam, Jetsam and the Science of Ocean Motion*
8.5	*Skyscraper*
9.5	*The Ultimate Weapon: A Race to Develop the Atomic Bomb*

Accelerated Reader (AR) Reading Levels—Fiction

AR Level	Book Title
3.5	*Night of the Howling Dogs*
3.6	*Agnes Parker... Staying Cool in Middle School*
3.6	*Eggs*
3.7	*The Entertainer and the Dybbuk*
3.8	*Open Court*
3.9	*A Crooked Kind of Perfect*
4.1	*Fairest*
4.1	*Pete and Fremont*
4.2	*One-Handed Catch*
4.2	*Framed*
4.2	*Toby Wheeler Eighth-Grade Benchwarmer*
4.3	*Missing Magic*
4.3	*Johnny and the Bomb*
4.3	*Beowulf: A Hero's Tale Retold*
4.4	*The Miraculous Journey of Edward Tulane*
4.4	*Magpie Gabbard and the Quest for the Buried Moon*
4.4	*Gossamer*
4.5	*The Book of Story Beginnings*
4.5	*Jeremy Fink and the Meaning of Life*
4.6	*The Golden Dream of Carlo Chuchio*
4.6	*On the Wings of Heroes*
4.7	*Middle School Is Worse than Meatloaf*
4.8	*Vanishing Act: Mystery at the U.S. Open*
4.8	*Football Genius: A Novel*
4.8	*Me and the Pumpkin Queen*
4.8	*Encyclopedia Brown: Cracks the Case*
4.9	*Cracker: The Best Dog in Vietnam*

4.9	*Schooled*
4.9	*Out of Patience*
5	*The Silver Donkey*
5	*What-the-Dickens: The Story of a Rogue Tooth Fairy*
5	*The Mailbox*
5.1	*The Traitor's Gate: A Novel*
5.1	*The Invention of Hugo Cabret*
5.2	*Diary of a Wimpy Kid*
5.2	*Theodosia and the Serpents of Chaos*
5.2	*A Dog for Life*
5.2	*Emma-Jean Lazarus Fell Out of a Tree*
5.5	*The Castle Corona*
5.6	*The Mysterious Benedict Society*
5.6	*George's Secret Key to the Universe*
5.7	*The Mysterious Edge of the Heroic World*
5.8	*Miss Spitfire: Reaching Helen Keller*
5.8	*The Legend of Bass Reeves*
5.9	*The Wednesday Wars*
6.1	*Atherton: The House of Power*
6.3	*Chaucer's Canterbury Tales*

Index

About the Author

BETH McGUIRE is the school librarian at Fannett-Metal School District in Willow Hill, Pennsylvania. She has worked with elementary, middle, and high school students, teachers, and community members for four years since earning her master's degree in library science from Clarion University of Pennsylvania. She also earned a bachelor of science in education, secondary education English, from Clarion University. Active reading is just as important as active librarianship to Beth. She has served on the Pennsylvania School Library Association state journal Editorial Review Board for Learning and Media and is co-director of the Southern Pennsylvania Information Exchange Source, a member of the Technology Advisory Board for the Lincoln Intermediate Unit, a trainer for PA Department of Education programs, and a grant evaluator for the Library and Technology Services for the state of Pennsylvania. Beginning in 2008, she has served as the secretary for the Pennsylvania School Librarians Association.